CONTEMPORARY GLASS ENAMELING

Fusing with Powders, Paints, and Frit

by Kay Bain Weiner

First Edition:
Published in the United States by
Eastman Publishing
7447 Via de Fortuna, Carlsbad, CA 92009

ISBN 0-9720523-1-3

Library of Congress Control Number: 2004113813

ON THE PREVIOUS PAGE:

Janet Zambai

The panel was deeply carved by sandblasting clear glass. Enamel paint was applied with an airbrush, and the panel was then fired.

DEDICATION AND KUDOS

This book is dedicated to the glass artists who constantly strive to venture beyond the boundaries of their art to create the extraordinary.

Special thanks go to my friend of many years, Peggy Karr, whose inspirational enamel art has become world-famous.

I am sincerely grateful to Diana Rodriguez for her photographic and graphic art contribution and tireless efforts toward the production of this book.

I extend my deepest gratitude to Ann Valsasina for her editing expertise.

Finally, I extend my admiration and appreciation to all the hot glass artists and instructors who have contributed their creativity, knowledge, and work to this book. You have all inspired me, and I treasure your friendship.

Some of the photographed works in progress and completed pieces were created by my students under my guidance and direction. These photographs are used to illustrate various glass enameling techniques. I am grateful to my students for giving me the opportunity to use them.

Contents

Foreword — 10

Introduction — 12
Beginnings — 13
Resurgence of Interest — 13
New Horizons — 14
About This Book — 14

CHAPTER ONE
What Is Enameling? — 17
Glass Enameling — 17
The Evolution of Enameling — 18
The Twentieth Century — 20
Production of Fusible Glass — 22
Today's Glass — 22

CHAPTER TWO
Enamel Powders, Paints, and Glass — 23
Types of Enamels — 23
Enamel Powders — 26
Liquid Enamel Painting — 27
Types of Glass — 28
  Fusible Glass
  Textured Glass
  Float Glass
Tin Scope Lamp — 32

CHAPTER THREE
Preparatory Steps — 35
Before Starting Work — 35
Cutting Glass — 35
Cleaning Glass — 35
Light Source — 35
Clean Water and Paper — 36
Prepairing Molds and Shelves — 36
  Sifting Kiln Wash
  Brushing Kiln Wash
  Coating a Metal Mold
  Removing Kiln Wash
Fiber Paper — 39
Bas Relief Patterns — 40
Lava Cloth — 42

CHAPTER FOUR
Creating Stencils and Sifting Enamel Powders — 43
Getting Ready To Work — 43
Making Stencils — 43
  Stencil Supplies
  Patterns
Enameling and Sifting Supplies — 48
Sifting Enamels — 48
  Stencil One
  Subsequent Stencils
  Shading
  Detailing with Line Sifters

Gadgets for Sifting Enamels 51
Designing Tools 52

CHAPTER FIVE
Mixing and Applying
Enamel Paints 56

Liquid Enamels 56
  Tracing a Pattern
  Use of Stencils

Various Enamel Paints 57

Paint Mediums 58
  Water-based Binders
  Oil-based Binders

Fuse Master Enamels 58

Unique Glass Colors 60

Painting Washes Using Liquid Enamels 60

Outlining Paints 60
  Mixing Outlining Paint
  Outlining with Pen or Bottle
  Felt Tip Pens
  Gold and Silver Outlines
  Glassline

Steps before Firing 64

More about Painting 64

CHAPTER SIX
Brush Types and Strokes 65

About Brushes 65

Brush Composition 66

Brush Lengths and Sizes 66

Brushes for Glass 67

Brush Shapes 67

Loading the Brush 67

Flat Brushes 67
  Shader Brush

  Wash Brush
  One-stroke Brush
  Dagger Striper Brush
  Angular Shader Brush
  Rake Brush
  Fan Brush

Round Brushes 71
  Ultra-round Brush
  Liner Brush
  Filbert Brush
  Miracle Wedge® Brush
  Spotter Brush
  Tight Spot Detailer Brush
  Stippler Brushes
  Deerfoot Stippler Brush

Brush Care 74

Learn How 74

Bridge Support 75

CHAPTER SEVEN
Unique Enamel Paint
Applications 76

Innovative Techniques 76

Sponges 78
  Sea Sponges
  Synthetic Sponges
  Explore the Possibilities
  Sponging over a Grid

Stamps 80
  Noncolored Ink Pad
  Rubber Rollagraph

Brayers 80

Foil or Paper 80

Paint and Sift 81

Comb or Texturizing Tool 81

Cardboard Stamp 81

Sgraffito 83

Twine or String   83
Reverse Monoprint   83
Applicator-tipped Bottles   84
Credit Cards and Paint Scrapers   84
Texturizing with Feathers   85
Painting Knife   86
Airbrushing Glass   86
Looking Ahead   86

CHAPTER EIGHT
Additions and Inclusions
for Special Effects   **87**
A Variety of Products   87
Luster and Pattern Decals   88
   Carefree Luster™ Decals
   Pattern Decals
   How To Use Decals
Sheet Copper   90
Mica Powders and Flakes   90
Liquid Gold and Silver Paint   91
   Applying Metallics
   Using an Outlining Pen
Metal Wire   92
Gold, Silver, and Copper Leaf   92
Glues and Adhesives   93
Dichroic Glass   93
Miscellaneous Material   93
Fine Luster Powders   94
Bubbles   94

CHAPTER NINE
Color Selection   **95**
The Importance of Color   95

Warm Colors / Cool Colors   96
Color Perspective   96
Color Wheel   97
   Primary Colors
   Secondary Colors
   Tertiary Colors
   Complementary Colors
   Analogous Colors
   Monochromatic Colors
   Dominant Color
Color Illusions   99
   Color Intensity
   Color Relationships
   Color Facts
The "Color" of White   100
Animal Prints   102
Chemistry and Color   102
   Chemical Color Changes
   Compatibility Changes
   Reactions between Colors
Studying Color   103

CHAPTER TEN
Molds   **104**
Types of Molds   104
Ceramic Molds   104
   Greenware
   Plates
Pate De Verre   106
Metal Molds   106
Stacking   107
Fiber Board Molds   108
Wet Pack or Moist Pack   109
Mold Compounds   110

CHAPTER ELEVEN
Firing Enamel Projects   **112**

General Information   112

Firing Projects 12″ or Under   112
Manually Operated Kilns
Firing a Kiln with Digital Controls

Firing Using a Medium   114

Annealing   114

Enamel Firing Stages   115

Important Firing Tips   116

Troubleshooting Firing Problems   116
Glass Bubbles
Cracking
Factors Affecting Firing Results

Facts about Slumping   117

Overfiring   118

Bubbles   118

Cleaning the Finished Project   119

Devitrification   119

Removing Baked-on Kiln Wash   120

CHAPTER TWELVE
Kilns   **121**

Kiln Selection   121

Types of Power   121

Manual Controllers   121

Digital Controllers   122

More about Controllers   122
Infinite Switches
Simple Digital Controllers
Professional Digital Controllers

Top and Side Heating Elements   124

Top Elements
Side Elements
Combined Elements

Top Loading Kilns   124

Front Loading Kilns   124

Optional Accessories   125

CHAPTER THIRTEEN
Safety in the Work Area   **126**

Put Safety First   126

Heat and Fire Safety   126

Glass Safety   127

Protective Clothing and Accessories   127

General Precautions   128

Additional Advice   129

CHAPTER FOURTEEN
Artist Profiles   **130**

Coming to Terms with Glass   **153**

Additional Resources   **159**

References   **160**

Manufacturers   **162**

Contributors   **164**

Biography   **167**

Foreword

Techniques for heat-forming crushed glass into useful and decorative forms have been around for a couple of thousand years, but it is only since the 1980s that this art form has truly flourished. During the last 20-some years, the use of colored glass powders as an expressive art form has taken on a life of its own. From its contemporary roots in the copper enameling arena and the explosion of interest in the kiln-formed sheet glass process, we are seeing glass used in ways never before imagined.

It is only fitting that Kay's 13th book be on the subject of glass enameling. She started working with glass enamels in the 1960s. Her fascination with art glass grew with the blossoming stained glass movement of the '70s and '80s. Kay's solid foundation in design and the fundamentals of art helped her become a highly regarded teacher. Her presence at all of the major art glass programs, trade shows, and educational events has made her a fixture of the industry. Kay's boundless energy is paralleled only by her seemingly limitless creative vision. She is continually pioneering new innovations in whatever process she embraces.

This book is but another milestone in her long and illustrious career. The entire art glass—no, make that the entire ART—community will benefit from her ability to consolidate the wide subject of glass enamels into this insightful and comprehensive volume. Thanks, Kay.

Keep a Warm Kiln,

Gil Reynolds

Gil Reynolds

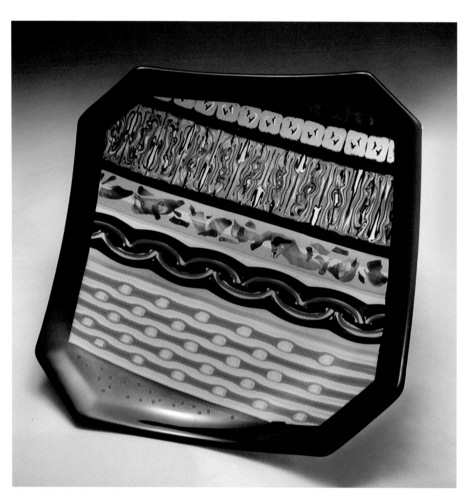

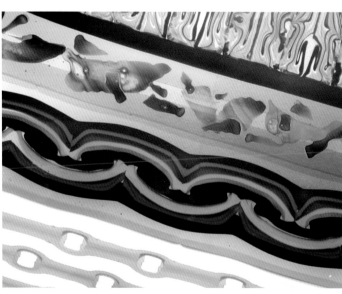

Introduction

"That last thing that we discover in writing a book, is to know what to put at the beginning."
— *Blaise Pascal*

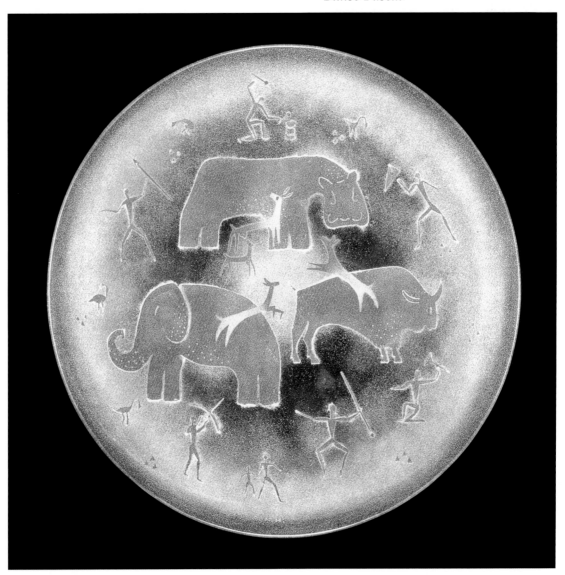

Maurice Heaton

In the mid-1960s, Heaton was considered a pioneer in glass enameling technique. This plate with a primitive motif marked the beginning of a new trend in hot glass art—a field that has mushroomed into a vigorous industry. Permission for use of this photograph from the Corning Museum of Glass.

BEGINNINGS

I first became fascinated with glass enameling in the mid-1960s and have watched its phenomenal growth over the years. I'm delighted to see that awareness of glass enamels is now at an all-time high. This new wave of interest in enameling techniques has ignited the imagination of glass artists who are seeking new artistic horizons to explore.

My own involvement with glass enameling and fusing became serious in the 1960s when I studied in New York with the prominent glass artist and designer Maurice Heaton, well known for his extraordinary achievements in glass enameling. But, although my interest in enameling continued, as an artist I found myself drawn to express my creativity through other glass art techniques.

RESURGENCE OF INTEREST

Little did I realize that my enthusiasm for glass enameling would once again emerge full force—fueled this time by my admiration for the accomplishments of my friend Peggy Karr. Today her name is synonymous with fused glass tableware, and her designs and art objects are highly prized by collectors.

She began fusing glass in 1983 and dreamed of mass-producing her enameled glassware. Through exploration and ingenuity, she refined her technique to a science. Her passion for glass enameling turned her artistry into a major manufacturing operation.

Robert Leatherbarrow

The panel shown here was created by sifting fine enamel powders onto multiple layers of glass. It was fired six times to produce this dramatic effect.

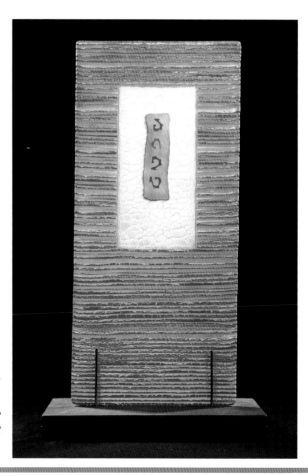

NEW HORIZONS

My book *Glass Enameling,* written in 1996, was published shortly before Uroboros Glass and Bullseye Glass began manufacturing fine powder forms of glass frit that can be used for enameling. So although that book contains information about other companies that were, and still are, producing glass enamels and paint, the subsequent enormous growth in the art glass industry indicates that an updated version could be extremely useful. My original book on glass enameling is still available, however, and contains photos, patterns, and instructions.

Writing this new book has been a fascinating and awe-inspiring experience and has allowed me to meet glass craftspersons from around the globe who have explored and developed exciting new concepts in the art of glass enameling.

ABOUT THIS BOOK

There are now many exciting venues of hot glass art. However, this new book focuses on the art of glass enameling—an overview of which appears in Chapter One.

There are various types of enamels and glass available. Chapter Two discusses the dry enamel powders and liquid paints

Robert Schmidt and Karen Tam

In a technique similar to mosaic, the artists use enamels to "grout" between the cut glass pieces. The decorated glass is then fired in the kiln.

that can be used, as well as compatible base glass.

I have offered some preparatory steps in Chapter Three that should be followed to successfully complete enameling projects.

In Chapter Four, which deals with creating stencils for sifting enamel powders, you will learn how to produce precise designs in enamels. Some ideas are presented for using household items and tools for sifting and for creating textures and patterns in the powders.

Another method of decorating glass is to paint with liquid enamels. Chapter Five gives step-by-step instructions for painting and mixing formulas.

Chapter Six discusses types of brushes and brush strokes to achieve painterly effects.

For the more adventuresome, Chapter Seven describes unique methods of applying enamel paint, such as using sponges or rubber stamps.

Discussed in Chapter Eight are additions and inclusions used by some of the more creative glass enamel artists. Many of these items will add just that special touch to your glass enamel concept.

Many glass artists will benefit from the information in Chapter Nine regarding color. Having an understanding of color relationships can transform a mediocre art piece into a dynamic creation.

Sagging and drape molds, discussed in Chapter Ten, are important for creating

Michael Dupille

This clever wall piece is shaped like a golf tee with a golf ball on top. Reflected in the ball is an image of Tiger Woods. The sifted enamel technique was used to create intricate details.

tableware and other projects. Included is information regarding mold material and how to make different molds appropriate for enameling.

Chapters Eleven and Twelve instruct you on essentials of firing glass enamels using manual and computerized kilns. Kiln know-how can make the difference between success and failure. Firing your projects is the final step, and often it is necessary to fire your glass several times to achieve your artistic vision. Various types of kiln controllers are described.

The safety tips in Chapter Thirteen are probably the most important of all the instructions given in this book. I strongly urge you to read and follow the advice.

Artist Profiles (Chapter Fourteen) gives you an insight into the imagination of various artists who work with enamels. The photos illustrate the versatility of the medium and the wide range of diverse projects possible with enamel powders and paints.

Following Artist Profiles, you will find a glossary of terms that might be helpful.

Even as you read this book, new developments and technology in the hot glass industry are taking place. With time, these could significantly change or modify the instructions in this text.

While the trend toward hot glass art escalates, and these new enameling products and techniques appear in the glass market, I look forward to exploring exciting new glass art frontiers.

Whether you are a beginner or an experienced glass artist, whatever your style, from traditional to abstract, I hope this text will serve as a useful resource on the art of glass enameling. May you experience the joy of exploring this wondrous art form and be inspired to experiment and express your artistic visions in a new hot glass arena.

What Is Enameling?

GLASS ENAMELING

In the heat of a kiln's fire, a phenomenon occurs when layers of glass and colors miraculously unite. The marvel of glass enameling is achieved through the transformation of glass granules fusing into glorious pools of color. The enamels are vividly colored glass powders or paints that are fired permanently onto glass.

Kathleen Sheard

This massive glass mural incorporates powders and frit to create sections that have been collectively fired 56 times.

**Designed by Peggy Karr
Fabricated by Peggy Karr Glass,
Inc.**

This intricately designed glass butterfly plate is an example of the technique of sifting enamel powders through a series of hand-cut stencils.

THE EVOLUTION OF ENAMELING

Throughout the centuries, glass has presented an esthetic challenge to the glass artisan. Traditionally glassmaking was regarded as an ancient, sophisticated medium that was the province of important artists. Inspired by this marvelous material with its jewel-like appearance, early craftsmen began incorporating glass into art objects destined for the church, the nobility, and other wealthy patrons.

Enameling on metal is a technique thousands of years old. It may have been discovered accidentally when melted sand and clay fused onto iron implements.

The people of many civilizations have recognized its beauty and utility, including the Chinese, the Greeks, the Indians, the Romans, and the Celts. Most of the known decorative techniques that we are aware of were invented by artisans of the Roman era, while the elaborate Byzantine enamels of the tenth century are still regarded by some as the finest examples of this art form. It was probably the beauty of enamels on metal that led artisans to experiment with firing enamels on glass.

The history of glass decorating from the eighth century through the fourteenth century focuses on the Islamic world of the Middle East, where quality colorless glass, fired-on enamel colors, and gilding techniques were developed. Egypt introduced lustrous metallic effects on both pottery and glass. Glass was made in India as early as the fifth century B.C., but the industry was not established there until the Mughal period (1526 to 1857). Mughal glass was often gilded or enameled in floral patterns.

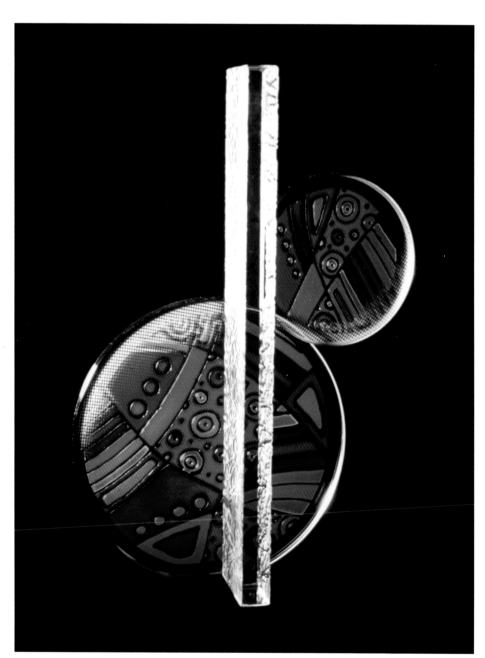

Steve Maddy

Low fire enamels are the specialty of this artist. Using clear glass as the base, he creates a series of dramatic coordinating sculptures.

Avery Anderson

The artist combines several glass techniques with glass enameling. Intricately designed layers of glass are fused in several kiln firings.

In the nineteenth century, glassmaking was influenced by rapid advances in technology and the rediscovery and adaptation of older methods. At that time, a resurgence of interest in glass art occurred. Enamels and stains were applied to glass objects—a trend that coincided with the revival of stained-glass windows. Although manufacturing processes are more sophisticated today, the components of glass have remained almost the same.

THE TWENTIETH CENTURY

We can credit Maurice Heaton with the 1947 rejuvenation of the process of fusing crushed crystals of enamel to the undersurface of glass. Years later he adapted the technique to accommodate the fusing of colored enamels between as many as six layers of glass.

In the 1980s, Peggy Karr, who has become one of the foremost enamelists in the country, began mass-producing a distinctive line of glass enamel dinnerware and accessories. She can also be credited with influencing many glass artists to pursue working with glass enamels and making the public aware that glass art can be functional as well as beautiful.

New manufacturing technology, however, has led to an impressive array of unique

Cathy Coverley

This panel is a frit cast mosaic piece made from many different sizes of glass frit. The frit is laid into a glass framework, working from front to back. The glass is then fired all at once to create a panel 3/8" thick. The award-winning glass artist uses this technique to create intricate details.

sheet glass and related glass products, as well as state-of-the-art equipment, that challenges the serious glass artist.

Today, glass enameling involves hand-decorating glass surfaces with vibrantly colored granulated glass or liquid enamel paints. The glass is then fired in a kiln in a range of temperatures depending on the number of glass pieces and type of enamels or powders used. The recent hot glass movement and the availability of fusible glass have brought forth a profusion of innovative fired glass techniques. However, applying enamels on glass remains a distinct and unique art form.

PRODUCTION OF FUSIBLE GLASS

In the mid-1970s, Bullseye Glass of Oregon was the first to begin producing a unique type of art glass, as well as powders and frit, with qualities that make the glass ideal for fusing. Soon after, Uroboros Glass, also located in Oregon, introduced its own line of fusible glass products. The availability of fusible compatible glass opened possibilities for decorating and kiln-forming glass without the use of enamels. Interest in hot glass escalated, and kiln companies began manufacturing kilns made specifically for melting glass.

Currently the hot glass artist has an extensive variety of transparent and opaque lead-free glass powders, frit, and liquid paints from which to select. These products are made by several manufacturers in a variety of mesh sizes and colors, along with compatible base glass. Increasing interest has brought with it an impressive growth in the manufacture of all art glass and related supplies.

TODAY'S GLASS

In the last few years, several glass factories in the United States have begun producing fusible glass with specific and unique qualities.

The contemporary glass artist has the advantage of being able to use a selection of diverse machinery, kilns, and tools, many of which were not available until recently. These products have opened creative paths never before traveled. Design and technical hot glass concepts that once could only be imagined can now be easily and conveniently achieved through modern-day technology.

Further developments in the hot glass art industry look promising and will be welcomed by innovative glass artists ready to step beyond today's boundaries.

I hope you will see the potential of glass enameling and that this book will help bring you to a new creative level. We can only imagine the glass art that is yet to come.

Enamel Powders, Paints, and Glass

TYPES OF ENAMELS

This book focuses primarily on liquid enamels and enamel powders that are fired permanently onto glass. Either liquid or dry powder enamel techniques can be used to create tableware, dividers, window panels, tiles, jewelry, lamp panels, box tops, table tops, and other items.

Juanita Niemeyer

This intricately decorated screen was produced using single-thick window glass painted with enamels manufactured by Unique Glass Colors. Also used was their 24k gold outline enamel to enhance the design.

Tony Glander

This vibrant abstract glass enamel panel features a silk-screened photo image.

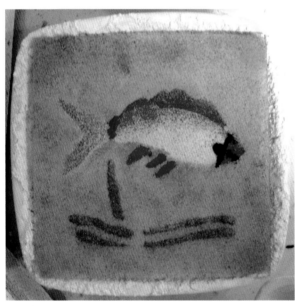

The three unfired 6" x 6" tiles pictured here suggest possible subjects for tiles. Glass tiles are appropriate to use on bathroom or kitchen counters, or on the walls of a child's room. Photos courtesy of Lighthouse Stained Glass, Venice, CA.

There are three categories of enamels: glass stainer colors, enamel powders, and liquid enamels. Low fire glass stainer colors have been used for centuries for traditional painting, most evident in church windows. There have been, however, more recent glass enamels developed in the mid-twentieth century.

Some of these newer enamel powders, available in opaques and transparents, can be sifted onto glass; others can be mixed with an assortment of water- or oil-based mediums for hand-brushing, silk-screening, or airbrushing onto glass. Also available are an assortment of liquid enamel paints packaged in jars and applicator bottles.

ENAMEL POWDERS

Enamel powders, referred to by some manufacturers as "fine frit," are usually 80-mesh (lead-free) and can be sifted onto clear or colored glass, as described in Chapter Three. Enamel powders manufactured by Bullseye Glass, Uroboros Glass, and Thompson Enamel have an expansion rate compatible with fusible and float glass and mature between 1450°F and 1550°F. For special effects, enamel powders can be sifted through a variety of stencils or nontraditional implements. Most of these enamel powders are sifted and fired on one piece of glass or laminated between two layers of glass.

One of the most prevalent uses of the sifted dry powder technique is for the creation of tableware. For many such projects, molds are used to sag the glass. Laminating enamels secures the colors, and when fired and annealed properly, the tableware can be dishwasher-safe. However, the same technique is also used to create jewelry, tiles, panels, and other art objects that may not require lamination.

When purchasing fine powders to use in enamel work, you may find that there is a slight variation in grain size. For instance, Uroboros fine powder size ranges between 0.13 mm and 0.25 mm, whereas Bullseye fine powder size is under 0.2 mm. Some manufacturers' powders are designated as 90 or 96 COE. (See "Types of Glass," in this chapter.)

Dry sifted enamels can be laminated between two pieces of glass. The panel illustrates the appearance before firing. Photos courtesy of Lighthouse Stained Glass, Venice, CA.

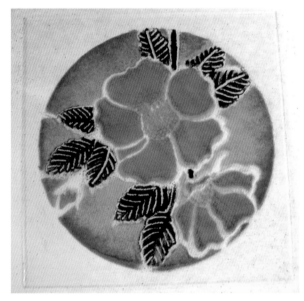

Enamel powders were sifted through several stencils to create this flower motif.

LIQUID ENAMEL PAINTING

In recent years, new types of liquid enamels have become available that offer the opportunity to create different effects by applying them with artist brushes, sponges, brayers, rubber stamps, or an airbrush. You will find these techniques fun to explore, and you will be amazed at the exciting results. Refer to the back of the book for a listing of the manufacturers of various enamels. "How-To" instructions for painting are covered in Chapter Five.

You may develop a preference for the painting method over the sifting system. However, you will find that they each have advantages. You do not need to be apprehensive about painting free hand. Your patterns can be placed under the glass, traced, and used as a guide. The liquid brush-on technique also enables you to paint intricate pattern details, such as a face or the veins of a leaf.

The brush-on enamel technique can be accomplished by using ready-made liquid enamels, such as Unique Glass Colors, or by mixing Fuse Master enamel powders with a water-based or an oil-based medium. Working with a water-based medium is easier. Fine enamel powders mixed with an oil-based medium take several hours to dry. However, the consistency of the mixture is similar to that of acrylic paints and might be preferred by some. All enamels can be painted on single- or double-thick glass or laminated between two single-thick pieces of glass.

Kay Bain Weiner

The cheetah panel is an example of painting using opaque liquid enamels.

A pattern is placed under the glass to use as a guide for outlining and painting. Photo courtesy of Unique Glass Colors.

TYPES OF GLASS

Glass suitable for creating enamel projects includes fusible glass (clear or colored) and float glass. These glasses are available in several thicknesses. Your choice of base glass will depend on the manufacturers of the glass enamel powders you are planning to use.

Fusible Glass

Often fusible glass is marked either 90 or 96 COE. The coefficient of expansion (COE) refers to the rate of expansion and contraction when the glass is heating and cooling. When glass becomes liquid, its rate of flow is referred to as its "viscosity level."

Various manufacturers may produce glass having the same COE; however, the viscosity and the melting and annealing points of the glass may differ by manufacturer. Therefore, it is wise to purchase glass and powders produced by the same manufacturer. For instance, use Bullseye fine powders if you are using Bullseye base glass (fusible clear or colored). Uroboros manufactures both 90 and 96 COE fusible glass, powders, and frit. Thompson Enamel manufactures several different types of enamel powders that are compatible with certain types of glass, including float glass. Make sure you purchase the appropriate powder for the glass. An experienced hot glass supplier can advise you.

Steve Maddy

Here, 1" clear glass is dramatically enhanced by low fire glass enamels.

Brock Craig

Using geometric pieces of silver and gold leaf between layers of fusible clear glass helped to create an illusion of depth. The metal squares appear to be floating over the black base glass. See Chapter Eight for details on metal inclusions.

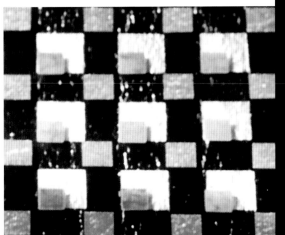
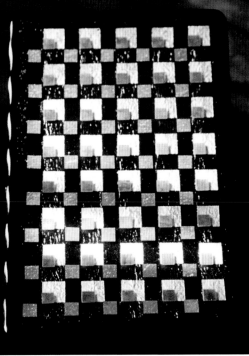

Glass that is 90 COE might be more readily available through retailers since it has been manufactured several years longer than 96 COE. At this time, several other glass manufacturers have started producing fusible glass: Wasser Glass, Armstrong Glass, Spectrum Glass, and Youghiogheny Glass; and some of the manufacturers of fusible glass are producing sheet glass in different thicknesses.

It is possible that two different manufacturers' glass may not be compatible even if they have the same COE. On the other hand, glasses with different COEs may be fusing compatible. Keep in mind, however, that the quantity of enamel powders used on most simple glass projects is limited and may not be affected by COE or viscosity.

Textured Glass

When selecting glass for use in your project, consider that there is some clear fusible glass that has inclusions, such as seeds or line striations, that will remain in the glass when it is fired.

For the more experienced hot glass artist, there are many patterns of fusible textured clear glass that can sometimes be used to a design advantage. Firing two textured surface glasses together could result in an interesting pattern. For instance, two pieces of ribbed glass, pattern sides together and placed with

the ribbed pattern running in opposite directions, could offer an imaginative design concept.

As you become more familiar with enameling, you will find that there are many materials and ideas to explore.

For tableware, two layers of standard 1/8" thick glass is recommended. If you are using clear glass 1/4" to 3/4" thick for table tops or room dividers, one layer is adequate.

If you are working with the thin fusible glass, your project could incorporate three or four layers of this thinner glass.

Float Glass

Many of the commercial enamelists who create tableware use float glass. Float glass, also known as window glass, can be successfully used with 90 COE powders, such as Thompson Enamel powders.

In recent years, much of the clear glass produced in the United States is made by

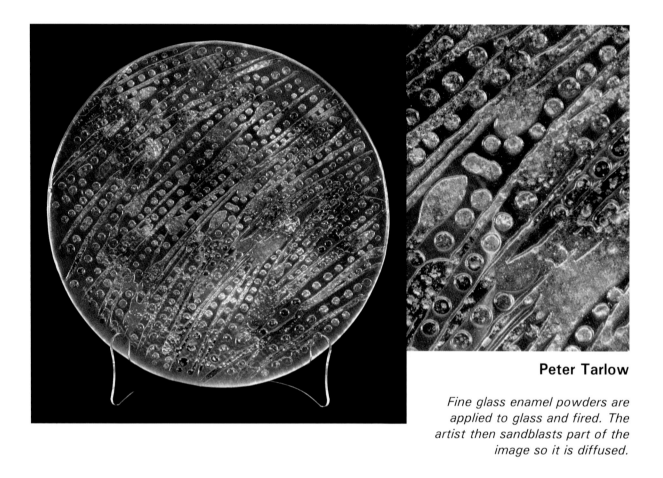

Peter Tarlow

Fine glass enamel powders are applied to glass and fired. The artist then sandblasts part of the image so it is diffused.

a float process. As molten glass flows from the furnace, it floats across the surface of a bath of molten tin. The temperature is lowered as the glass moves across the tin. When the glass becomes rigid, it leaves the tin surface and passes through an annealing oven. The result is a smooth sheet of glass with two completely different surfaces. During fusing, the tin side of the glass can slightly discolor the enamel glass colors, so you want to be careful to apply enamels only to the non-tin glass side. You can determine the tin side by using a tin scope, described on the following page.

Be aware that all float glass does not have identical characteristics. Various manufacturers' glass may vary in COE. However, if you are using only enamels on your base float glass, they are usually applied thinly enough to avoid causing stress breakage. If you are laminating float glass, make sure that the pieces are cut from the same sheet. Float glass is available in several thicknesses.

For larger projects, such as platters, use double-thick clear glass. After fusing, the lamination of two double-thick pieces of glass is equivalent to a 1/4" thickness. Projects such as jewelry, box tops, lamp panels, and sun catchers are usually made with a single layer of glass and enamel. Float glass is also ideal for producing large table tops or room dividers. You can buy float glass through glass shops.

TIN SCOPE LAMP

You can identify the tin side of float glass using a special battery detector lamp called a "tin scope." To use: In a darkened area, place the shortwave ultraviolet light window against the glass. The tin side will be foggy with a white haze. This haze may be difficult to distinguish at first, but with practice it will become easier to identify. It is important to apply enamels only to the clear side of float glass. The tin side will change the enamel colors slightly, giving them a yellowish cast. If you are using a second piece of glass on top, place the clear side facing the enamels. Tin scopes are available from some hot glass product suppliers.

A tin scope lamp enables the viewer to determine which is the tin (foggy) side of float glass. Photo courtesy of Fusion Glass Works, Newberg, OR.

Carmen Reynolds

Fuse Master Enamels were sifted onto the top of the glass, and then a comb was dragged through the enamel powder.

Kathleen Sheard

This artist meticulously assembles layer upon layer of glass, powders, and frit. The decorated glass is fired several times to create a dynamic impressionistic work of art.

Fabricated by Peggy Karr Glass, Inc.

A single 4″ circular glass disk was used to create this bird motif sun catcher. Fine enamel powders were sifted through hand-made cardboard stencils.

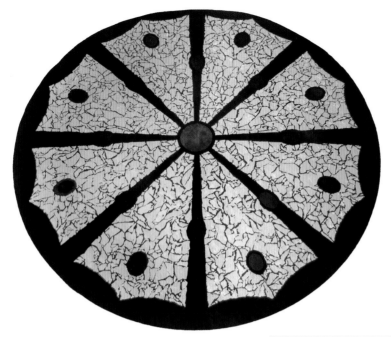

Brock Craig

The decorated glass is sandblasted and then decorated with shredded heavy gold foil. The foil is pulled apart with tweezers and reassembled like a puzzle. Oil medium was used to hold the foil in place.

Designed by Peggy Karr
Fabricated by Peggy Karr Glass, Inc.

The 3/8" thick table top was produced using dry enamel powders sifted through a series of hand-cut stencils.

34

Preparatory Steps

BEFORE STARTING WORK

These important and helpful steps should be read before you begin your enamel decorating. Also, it is essential to remember that you should use a mask or a respirator when working with glass enamels. Inhaling glass particles can cause silicosis, a serious lung disease.

CUTTING GLASS

If you are using a mold, the glass should be cut to the exact size of the mold. After the glass is cut, smooth away any rough edges with a grinder. If you want to design and create an abstract shape, the glass can be cut into an interesting design even if you

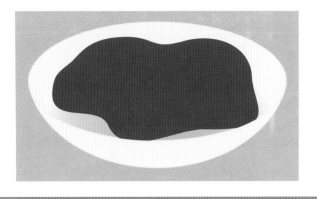

are using a conventional mold (as seen in the illustration on this page).

CLEANING GLASS

Wash glass in dish detergent and warm water, or scrub with a powdered cleanser (such as Comet), and rinse well. Dry the clean glass between newspapers or with a lint-free paper towel. Handle glass by the edges to avoid marring it with fingerprints. If you prefer, glass can be cleaned with denatured alcohol. Don't use rubbing alcohol because it contains oils. Window cleaners are not suitable because they contain silicones that make enamel colors crawl.

LIGHT SOURCE

It is helpful to use a light box when working with enamels because it enables you to apply the sifted and painted enamels evenly. If a light box is unavailable, lift the glass above the table surface by resting the edges on kiln posts or small cans. A light source placed underneath or near the glass will help you sift or paint the enamels more evenly, as seen in the picture at right.

Good lighting is essential when painting and decorating glass. Evaluate your needs, and choose the light best for your space. There are lamps with true day lighting especially manufactured with the artist in mind. They do not heat the work area, and they provide excellent lighting.

CLEAN WATER AND PAPER

Keep a container of clean water and some paper towels nearby when painting. When finished using a color, wipe the brush on a paper towel. Rinse the brush in the clean water before putting it into the next color.

After an enameling session, store leftover paints in containers, or use an aluminum foil cover. If the paint dries, it can be reconstituted with a few drops of water and medium.

PREPARING MOLDS AND SHELVES

All mold resists and primers are not created of the same materials. Be sure to inquire of your glass mold dealer if the molds you purchase require special treatment or resist products. For instance, some pate de verre molds come with special directions regarding the type of primer to use.

There are several methods of preparing a mold or a kiln shelf for firing. It is important to use a kiln separator (resist) in powder or liquid form or to use fiber paper before placing the decorated glass on the mold or shelf. This will keep melted glass from adhering to mold or shelf surfaces.

Apply shelf primer, also referred to as "kiln wash," on your shelves and kiln floor. The floor of your kiln should be painted with three or four coats of kiln wash. This preparation is necessary because otherwise enamel powders or frit could spill onto the floor during firing and melt a hole in the ceramic brick of the kiln. Never kiln wash the walls or lid of your kiln!

To sift dry kiln wash onto a mold, use a sifter or a confectioner's sugar shaker to coat the surface.

Sifting Kiln Wash

A powdered mold separator or kiln wash sifted onto the mold will prevent the glass from adhering to it. A large cardboard box can serve as a sifting area. Do not coat molds near decorated projects because particles of the separator can adhere to them.

To proceed:

1. If the molds have air holes, place toothpicks into the air holes to prevent them from filling with mold separator. Smaller, flatter molds do not require air holes.

2. Use a wire kitchen strainer, flour sifter, or confectioner's sugar shaker to sift kiln separator over the mold, and evenly

TIP TOP-IC
If you are mass producing, it is wise to cover all shelves and molds with several coatings of resist, even if you are also planning to use fiber paper in the molds.

cover the surface of the mold to a depth of approximately 1/16" to 1/8".

3. Remove the toothpicks.

4. Holding the decorated glass by the edges, center it on the mold or shelf. Carefully place the second piece of washed glass (if used) on top of the decorated piece. If using float glass, remember to place the glass tin side up. (See Chapter Two for tin details.)

Most kiln wash powder is relatively inexpensive and should be disposed of after one firing. Alumina hydrate, a powder resist, can be reused. It is costly, however, and may not be worth the difference in price.

Brushing Kiln Wash

Kiln wash can be mixed as follows: Use one part dry powder to one part water. Put powder into water. Mix gently to the consistency of light cream.

Use a soft-bristle brush (such as a haike brush) to apply four or five coats of kiln wash onto a shelf or mold.

Several coats of kiln wash can be applied to the mold with a soft haike brush.

After applying coats of mold release, smooth the surface with a soft cloth. Photo courtesy of Unique Glass Colors.

To proceed:

1. Load the brush and apply an even horizontal coat of kiln wash over the entire mold or shelf surface.

2. Wait a few minutes and then apply a vertical second coat.

3. Allow kiln wash to dry between coats.

4. Repeat procedure for the next two or three coats.

5. Allow the kiln shelf to air dry completely, or place it in a warm kiln at 350°F for an hour or two.

6. If dried coatings are uneven, take a cloth and lightly smooth the surface. Do this procedure outdoors, if possible, and be sure to wear a mask.

Coating a Metal Mold
Metal molds, usually made of stainless steel, cannot be coated in the same manner as ceramic molds. Stainless steel is one of the best mold materials to use when slumping glass over a form. During the cooling process, the metal contracts more than the glass. This makes it easy to separate the glass from the now slightly smaller metal mold. The following is one method of coating metal molds:

1. Heat the metal to approximately 400°F in your oven or kiln.

2. Using gloves or tongs, remove the

mold from the kiln and place it on a nonflammable surface, such as a kiln shelf.

3. Before the metal cools, spray the kiln wash onto the mold using an airbrush or spray bottle that will give you a nice, even, fine coat. However, if you are using a brush, make sure to apply the wash evenly. Because the metal is hot, the kiln wash dries before it has a chance to run.

4. Repeat the heating and spraying of the mold three to five times until the metal is not visible.

You do not need to coat the mold before each firing as long as the protective layers of kiln wash appear to be intact. This rule applies to all types of molds and kiln shelves.

An alternate method for coating metal molds is to sandblast the mold before coating so that the metal surface is more porous and will accept the liquid kiln wash easily either by brushing or by spraying.

Removing Kiln Wash

Kiln wash, if properly applied, can withstand several firings. However, if the kiln wash is peeling off, scrape off the old wash with a plastic putty knife or dry plastic scrubbing pad. Wear a dust mask to keep from inhaling particles. Work outdoors if possible. Clean up the area with a wet cloth immediately. You can now recoat the shelves.

FIBER PAPER

An alternative to kiln wash is fiber paper, which comes in various thicknesses from 1/32" to 1/3". Cut the fiber paper to size to fit under your project on a shelf or in a mold. Some fiber papers give off fumes when fired, so it is necessary to ventilate the kiln at the beginning of the firing or pre-firing. Fiber shelf paper lasts for several firings if handled carefully.

Fiber paper is a lightweight material. Some types are processed from aluminum silica fibers to withstand temperatures of up to 2300°F. The thicker the paper, the more kiln firings it will withstand. It acts as a separator when cut to fit a mold or a shelf. The finished glass will retain the surface texture of the fiber paper.

A wafer-thin heat-resistant fiber paper is also available and will help to release glass from the mold. It provides separation between kiln shelf or mold and glass in kiln firings up to 1600°F. Designed for use with drape molds, it makes a good buffer between glass and mold. However, this paper can be used only once.

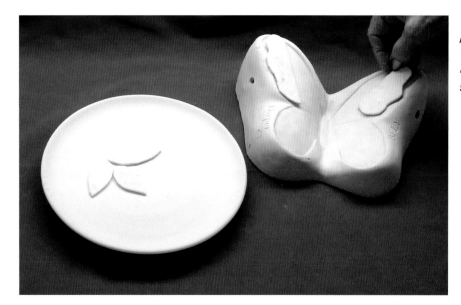

Thick fiber paper can be placed on the mold under the glass to create a bas relief effect in the fired glass.

BAS RELIEF PATTERNS

If you would like your finished glass projects to have an interesting bas relief pattern or texture on the back of the fired glass, here are some ideas:

On your mold or shelf, sift powder resist at least 3/8" deep. Press your fingertip evenly into the powder to create a circular texture. Alternate idea: Use a comb to rake a linear pattern into the sifted resist, or use any object such as a small bottle top to create an interesting pattern.

Another method of creating a bas relief is to use heavy (1/4" thick) fiber paper on the surface of the mold. Trace the pattern of a

TIP TOP-IC

Some fiber papers may require pre-firing to 1300°F in your kiln. Ask your supplier to advise you if your fiber paper needs pre-firing. Cut such paper to size and fire it in your kiln to 1300°F before using it under your project.

leaf, flower, or any shape that complements your design onto the fiber paper. Cut out the fiber paper design and place it in the prepared mold. Lay the decorated glass on top. Once fired, the glass will be raised with a bas relief design.

After firing, rinse off any remaining fiber paper with water after the glass has cooled.

Bruce Laughlin

The artist creates his own molds and adds a texture on the mold. This creates a bas relief in the fired glass.

By pressing a finger into sifted kiln wash, you can create a interesting pattern on the back of the fired glass.

LAVA CLOTH

Lava Cloth is a new fabric product that can be used as a separator for molds and shelves. Lava Cloth is a textured material that can impart a pattern onto a glass surface. Lava Cloth cuts easily with good scissors or a fabric roller knife. It is tan in color prior to firing, turning white after firing.

To proceed:
1. It is recommended that Lava Cloth be pre-fired according to the following schedule: Ramp at 500°F per hour to 1400°F. Then heat soak for 10 minutes. Slight shrinkage will occur with the first firing.

2. Cut Lava Cloth into a design, or cut it to fit a mold. It comes in several texture patterns, so you can use two or three different textures on one mold.

3. Place Lava Cloth directly on the firing surface.

4. Place glass on the Lava Cloth and fuse.

Lava Cloth does not stick to glass, kiln shelves, kiln brick, or fiber once it has cooled.

Lava Cloth is a fiberglass product with the standard warnings for fiberglass materials. Wear long-sleeved, loose-fitting clothing when handling any fiberglass material. Wash hands with soap and warm water after handling. A disposable mask designed for nuisance-type dusts may be advisable.

When fusing directly on Lava Cloth, glass will expand and then contract during the cooling down phase. Lava Cloth and fused glass MUST cool down to room temperature before they are separated; otherwise the Lava Cloth will not tolerate many firings, and it may even tear apart.

Lava Cloth comes in various textures. When the glass is fired on it, the cloth imparts a texture onto the glass.

Creating Stencils and Sifting Enamel Powders

GETTING READY TO WORK

Before working with enamels, be sure to read the preparatory steps regarding both lighting and the coating of molds and kiln shelves with resist. (See Chapter Three.)

MAKING STENCILS

There are many types of stencils, sifters, and nontraditional implements through which to sift enamel powders. To make precise designs on glass, such as nature

**Fabricated by
Peggy Karr Glass, Inc.**

Peggy Karr Glass, Inc. uses float glass to produce all of its tableware and art objects. The artists used hand-cut stencils and the sifting powder technique to create the designs on these platters and bowls.

A separate stencil is created for each color section of the pattern. This fruit pattern requires six separate stencils.

scenes or still life, I recommend that you create stencils. These will give you patterns to use for sifting dry enamels onto the appropriate areas of the glass. The techniques described here can be used for such items as tiles, tableware, panels, and jewelry.

Each color you use requires tracing and cutting a separate stencil for that color area. For example, if you are planning to use five colors on your project, you will need to create five separate stencils. A stencil can be used twice for shading a color such as in a leaf, bird, or flower.

Stencil Supplies
• Three to five sheets of stiff paper such as cardstock (file folders are suitable)
• Pattern
• Stencil knife
• Transfer paper (carbon paper)
• Crayons
• Ruler

Patterns
To create stencils, you need a suitable pattern, which you can either draw or find in a pattern book. (Dover Books has excellent stencil pattern books.) A suitable pattern should have a distinct

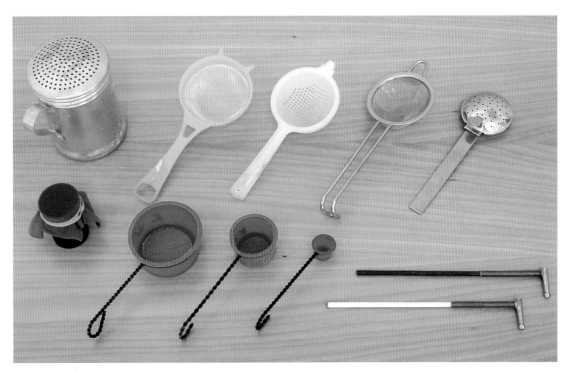

Various types of sifters can be used, depending on the size of the glass particles. Seen in the photo are commercial powder enamel sifters in several sizes, line sifters, and various tea sifters. You can also make your own sifters by using a film canister with a piece of stocking attached by a rubber band, as shown above, lower left.

One method of creating precise design sections is to sift fine powders through a stencil to create a single color segment of the pattern.

separation between design elements, or you may use a pattern with a heavy black line separating the elements. (See the illustrations on this page.)

To proceed:
1. Make a photocopy of the pattern, or trace it.

2. With crayons or colored pencils, color the original pattern to use as a guide.

3. Create stencils of stiff cardstock, or use file folders.

To make your stencils, use the following procedure:

• Cut each piece of cardstock 2″ larger than the size of the glass. For instance, for an 8″ piece of glass, cut the cardstock into a 10″ square.

• Using a ruler, measure the cardstock 1/2″ in from the edge on three sides.

Pattern with distinct separation of elements.

Pattern with a heavy black line separating the elements.

TIP TOP-IC
An alternate method of creating a stencil: Color the pattern with crayon. Use only four to six colors if you are a beginner. Then color photocopy the pattern onto cardstock as many times as you have colors. With a stencil knife, cut out only one of the colors on each piece of cardstock. Repeat this for each color you plan to use.

TIP TOP-IC
For opaque glass (glass which you cannot see through), use a light-colored transfer paper to transfer the entire design onto the glass. Colored transfer paper is available in sewing or art stores.

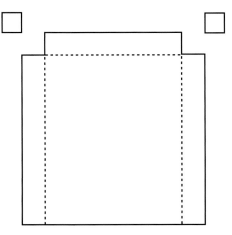

1. Cut out two corners of the cardstock before folding the three sides.

2. Make the scorelines and fold up edges.

3. To create each stencil, use carbon paper under the pattern. Trace each color section onto its own piece of cardstock.

4. Cut out each traced design section with a sharp stencil knife.

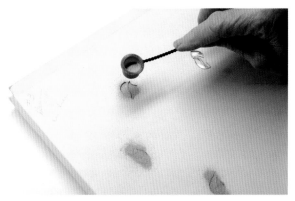

5. Fill the sifter with the desired enamel color. Starting with the stencil with the fewest cuts, gently tap the side of the sifter over the cut out areas.

6. To lift stencil, use two hands. Lift one side gently and then the other side.

Then, with a sharp instrument, such as the ruler's edge, make a scoreline. Notch out two corners at the top, as illustrated on the previous page.

• Save the cut-out corners to use as spacers (to be described later). Fold up the three sides at the scorelines. This makes the pattern easier to handle when sifting.

• Place transfer or carbon paper under the pattern to trace each color design section onto its designated piece of cardstock.

• With a sharp stencil knife, cut out each traced design. For reference, begin numbering the stencil with the fewest cuts first.

• Number each stencil in sequence, and mark each with the name of the design and the color to be used.

ENAMELING AND SIFTING SUPPLIES

• Fine enamel powders: opaque, 80-mesh, medium temperature, such as those manufactured by Uroboros Glass, Bullseye Glass, Thompson Enamel, and Fuse Master (340-mesh)

• Five or six enameling sifters or suitable tea strainers

TIP TOP-IC
Some glass enamelists prefer to spray the glass surface with a small amount of water-based medium or hair spray prior to or after sifting the enamel onto the desired area. This keeps the enamels intact.

• Fusible glass or float glass—See Chapter Two for detailed information on compatible glass and powders

• Several sheets of clean paper

• Prepared mold for tableware or other type of project (optional)

SIFTING ENAMELS

For convenience, place each enamel powder color in its own container—a small plastic jar will do nicely.

Stencil One
1. Place the colored pattern under the clear base glass or light-colored fusible glass. Use a light box if one is available. A light box enables you to judge enamel quantities more accurately.

2. Carefully place stencil one directly over the appropriate design area. Line up the stencil by looking down and checking against the pattern.

3. Spoon dry enamel into a small sifter.

4. Hold the sifter in one hand, and gently tap the sifter with a knife or your finger.

5. Cover the area with an even amount of enamel.

6. When lifting the stencil, use two hands on the upturned edges. First, carefully and slowly lift one side of the stencil about an inch; then remove the entire stencil.

7. Turn the excess enamel onto a piece of clean paper and funnel it back into its proper container. Try to keep your enamels clean.

8. Put previously cut cardboard spacers (the notched corners, as seen in the

Cookie cutters are versatile tools that can produce interesting designs.

illustration at right) on four edges of the glass, and leave them there until all stencils have been used. Spacers help to keep the enamel in place when the next stencil is placed on top or lifted.

Subsequent Stencils

Repeat the above procedure for each color with the remaining stencils. When you are finished, remove the spacers.

Shading

Experiment with shading when you are working with patterns such as fish, leaves, flower petals, water, birds, or clothing. Shading is important and will add more interest and dimension to your completed project.

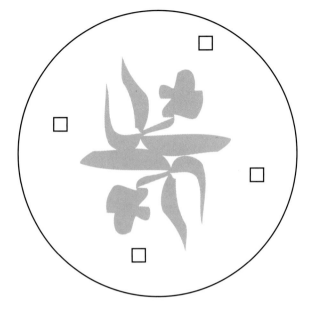

The cut pieces of cardboard will keep the stencils from touching the sifted enamels.

Using a line sifter can be helpful. The enamel powders are applied through a small opening at the end of the tool.

A variety of common kitchen and tool box implements can serve as stencils.

To shade a particular section, the stencil in use can be used twice—first to apply the dominant color and then to sift on a small amount of a different color for shading. You may end up with a mixed batch of enamels, but it may be easier than trying to place the stencil back over the sifted area.

If you are planning to laminate your project, as is suggested for all tableware, carefully put a clean layer of glass over the sifted enamels. It is now time to place your decorated glass onto a prepared shelf or

mold. Try to look directly over the mold so you can center your glass. Remember that a kiln wash resist or fiber paper should be applied to the mold and shelf prior to working with enamels.

Detailing with Line Sifters

To sift small dots or lines (such as seeds on a strawberry or veins on a leaf), a line sifter is a handy tool. The sifting hole comes with a 1/16" or 1/32" opening. Scoop enamel powder into the metal receptacle and quickly drop a dot or draw a line. Practice helps.

GADGETS FOR SIFTING ENAMELS

An array of nontraditional sifting tools can be used for sifting enamel powders. Stencils and design gadgets can be found in your kitchen, studio, or tool chest.

TIP TOP-IC

To preserve cardboard stencils, keep each group of stencils clipped together on skirt hangers for possible reuse. In the future, you might want to use one or two stencils from a group. For example, you could reuse a flower stencil portion for creating jewelry.

You'll find gadgets right in your kitchen, studio, or tool box that can help create unusual patterns in wet and dry enamels. The above items include a grapefruit cutter, a leather stamping tool, a wall texturizing comb, and various hair combs.

For interesting design concepts, the fine powders can be sifted through tea strainers, a drill disk, cut-off bottoms of plastic fruit and vegetable containers, paper or plastic doilies, brass or decorative lamp caps, commercial brass or plastic stencils (available in craft or paint stores), and small funnels.

Commercial stencils can be used, but they may be awkward to lift off the plastic, metal, or glass. If you do use them, you can attach small handles on either side made of small strips of copper foil or masking tape.

DESIGNING TOOLS

Designing implements can be adapted from a hair comb, a cookie or grapefruit cutter, a fork, or a rubber scraper. Commercial rubber or metal combing tools are available from paint, craft, and art stores.

A variety of combed patterns—wavy lines, scallops, crisscrosses, zigzags, and basket weaves—can be created using such items as combs or forks on painted liquid or sifted powder enamels.

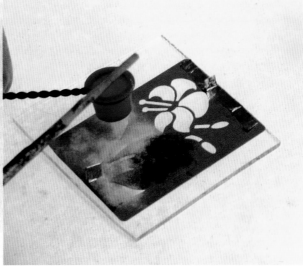

1. Small sifters are available for 80-mesh enamel powders. Commercial metal and plastic stencils can be purchased at art, craft, and paint stores.

2. A single metal stencil can be used. For different enamel colors, sections of the stencil can be covered with paper.

3. For ease in lifting, make a small handle on both ends of the stencil, using a strip of copper foil or masking tape.

4. Shown on the right is the commercial stencil used to create the sifted tile on the left.

 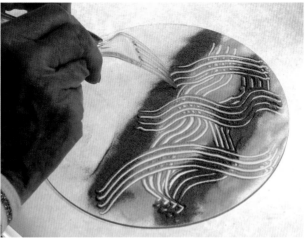

Combs or texturizing tools can be used to create designs in sifted or painted enamels. In the above photos, a plastic fork is being used to make a wavy, crisscross design.

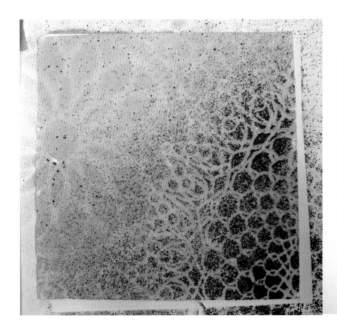 

Sifting through doilies can produce interesting designs. These photos show how effective doily patterns can be when used as a border surrounding the flowers. Photos courtesy of Lighthouse Stained Glass, Venice, CA.

Carmen Reynolds

Sifting enamel powders over ferns and foliage created a shadow image on this plate.

Details such as the waves in the lion's mane were accomplished by using a comb on the sifted dry powders.

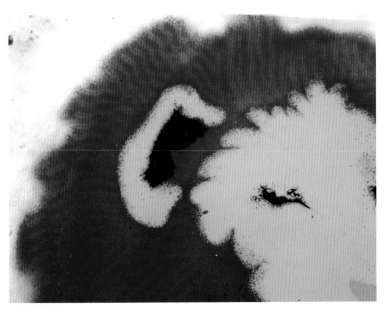

Mixing and Applying Enamel Paints

LIQUID ENAMELS

In recent years, new types of enamels have become available that offer the opportunity to create different design and texture effects by applying them with an artist's brush, a sponge, crinkled paper, an airbrush, brayers, rubber stamps, or other innovative means. (See Chapter Seven.)

Applying details such as a face, veins of a leaf, or shading is easily accomplished with the painting method. Your creativity might even inspire you to use both liquid and dry powdered enamels on the same project.

Tracing a Pattern
When using a painting technique, it is not necessary to create an individual stencil for each color. By placing a colored pattern under the clear glass, you can easily see the design, enabling you to paint details and blend the colors directly on the glass.

Nancy Duns Rich

Using a colored photo or illustration under the glass enables you to trace and paint a design such as the one on this tile.

Applying details and shading are easy to accomplish when using liquid enamels. Photo courtesy of Unique Glass Colors.

Use of Stencils

If you prefer to use stencils while painting enamels on glass, cover each paper stencil with a piece of clear contact paper before cutting out the design. This will keep the stencil patterns from getting wet and limp. A separate stencil can be used for each color in the design but is not required.

VARIOUS ENAMEL PAINTS

Described below are two manufacturers' techniques for mixing and applying their glass paints. Glass enamels are available at glass suppliers or ceramic shops.

The brush-on enamel technique can be accomplished by working with ready-to-use liquid enamels, such as Unique Glass Colors (to be described later in this chapter). Fuse Master's opaque enamel powders can also be sifted or mixed with a medium to create a liquid enamel. These enamels can be painted on most fusible glass, or on float glass, or they can be laminated between two pieces of glass. They are lead-free and dishwasher-safe when fired.

Some glass enamel powders, such as those manufactured by Reusche, mature at lower temperatures (1250°F to 1300°F) than many of the other glass enamels. Because of the their low-temperature capability, they can be fired onto three-dimensional vessels or fused glass art objects without disturbing the shape of a previously fired art concept.

PAINT MEDIUMS

Water-based mediums (binders) are easier to clean up, and they are used by many contemporary enamelists.

Water-based Binders
- Fuse Master Water Friendly Medium
- Gum arabic
- Honey
- Flat 7 Up
- Klyr Fire (Thompson Enamel)

Oil-based Binders
The following binders can be mixed with enamel powders, such as those made by Reusche and by Fuse Master. Fine enamel powders mixed with an oil-based medium take several hours to dry. The mixture has a consistency similar to that of acrylic paint.

Usable oil-based mediums include:
- Fuse Master Pine Oil Medium
- Clove oil
- Lavender oil
- Painting medium
- Squeegee oil

All glass paints are vitreous, which means that they contain the same elements found in glass. It is the medium that helps fuse the paint to the base glass during firing.

FUSE MASTER ENAMELS

Fuse Master paints come in opaque and transparent powder form. The 340-mesh size of the powder is fine enough to mix easily with a water- or oil-based medium. The lead-free opaques should be fired between 1450°F and 1550°F, depending on the project and the type of glass. Fuse Master also produces low fire transparent enamel powders. Do not mix opaques and low fire transparents together. All colors produced by this company can be mixed together to create an endless palette of hues.

To mix a water-based formula, proceed as follows:
1. Use a palette mixing knife or mixing stick on a clean piece of glass or a foam plate, or use small jars to mix the enamels according to the following formula:

- 1 level teaspoon of opaque high-fire powder
- 6 drops of Fuse Master Water Friendly Medium
- 1 teaspoon water

2. Stir the Water Friendly Medium and water into the enamel powder until the mixture has a milk-like consistency.

3. If necessary, stir in two or three more drops of water from an eyedropper. Be sure to use a palette knife or mixing stick (not a brush).

Peter McGrain

In a very distinctive style, the artist uses enamel paints that he mixes with a medium and fine powders. McGrain's clever use of shading demonstrates its importance in suggesting contours and dimension.

The enamels can be mixed to liquid consistencies that suit your painting needs. (See "Outlining Paints," in this chapter.) The medium burns away when the glass is fired.

UNIQUE GLASS COLORS

Paints produced under the brand name Unique Glass Colors are pre-mixed liquid enamels in a water-based medium. They are available in a wide range of opaque and transparent enamel colors and are formulated primarily for use on glass.

Stir each color well with a palette knife. Colors tend to settle in the jar and have to be stirred before and during use.

PAINTING WASHES USING LIQUID ENAMELS

For painting, select a soft round brush in size 2 or 4. Load the brush and "puddle" the paint on the desired area. To cover a large area (such as a background), apply the thinned color with an eyedropper, and use a brush to bring the color up to the outlines seen through the glass on your pattern. All colors dry slowly, and usually

TIP TOP-IC
To speed up the drying process between paint coats, use a personal fan, a warm hair dryer, or a heat gun.

brush marks level out, making one coat all that is necessary. If the color is too thick and the brush marks do not smooth out, add a few drops of water to the paint. You want the colors to flatten out to a smooth application.

If you wish to add shading, simply flow on the first color, then add a second and even a third color while the first is still wet; "squiggle" or "pat" the colors together. Alternate method: For other color mixes or for shadings, all colors can be mixed on the palette or in a container.

Unique Glass Colors and Fuse Master enamel paints have a firing range between 1475°F and 1550°F, but testing may be necessary to learn how the glass and enamels react in your kiln.

OUTLINING PAINTS

You can paint your design with or without an outline. If you choose to outline, there are several enamel manufacturers' products and methods to use for outlining your designs on the glass. The enamel paints are available in black, white, and several colors and come in plastic squeeze bottles (Unique Glass Colors and Glassline). These bottles come with fine metal tips. You can also fill your own plastic bottles, available from craft stores.

Apply Unique Glass Colors black enamel outline from a plastic squeeze bottle with a metal tip.

After the enamel outline has been applied, load the brush with the liquid enamel to paint in the outline. Shading the paint is extremely important in giving the flowers a touch of realism.

Enamel powders and paints will often change color slightly after firing. Photos courtesy of Unique Glass Colors.

Darlene Johnson and Judy Lee

This whimsical rabbit motif plate was enamel painted, using various brush types.

Mixing Outlining Paint

Prepare your own outlining paint by thinning any color with a small quantity of medium and water.

The mixed liquid enamel can be placed into a plastic bottle with a metal applicator or into an outlining pen. The metal outlining pen has a small receptacle attached which can be filled with an eyedropper, toothpick, or brush.

Outlining with Pen or Bottle

• Practice using the outlining pen or squeeze bottle on paper or scrap glass.

• When you feel comfortable using the pen or bottle, you can outline the entire pattern before or after it is painted.

• If it is necessary to stop briefly before the outline is complete, cover the metal tip of the bottle or the pen with a small piece of dampened paper towel. This will keep the tip from clogging.

• When the outline is complete, rinse the tip of the bottle and clean it out with a stiff brush; then affix the tip to a squeeze bottle containing water. A few squirts and it's clean. Clean pen with the supplied plunger or thin wire using water or an appropriate cleaner.

Felt Tip Pens

Thompson Enamel manufactures felt tip enamel pens with fine points. They are available in limited colors. These are ideal for outlining designs or drawing details on

Outlining pen.

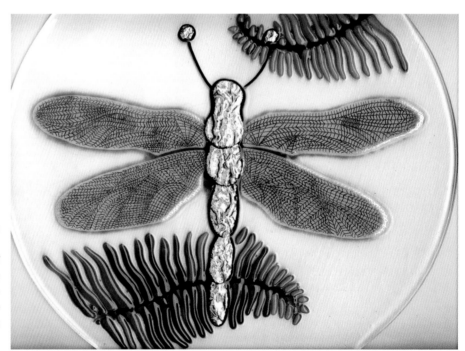

Jennifer Yalch

The intricately detailed veil wings of the dragonfly have been painted with silver paint, using an outlining pen.

TIP TOP-IC

To store paints: Once you have finished your painting project, cover the paints in containers. Because they dry quickly, they may need to be reconstituted when you want to use them again. If necessary, thin with water and stir thoroughly.

TIP TOP-IC

If you are not planning to fire your decorated project immediately, cover your work so it does not get dirty. A suggestion: Make a tent of aluminum foil to keep it clean.

glass. They fire between the temperatures of 1450°F and 1500°F. Since they fire at the same temperature as enamels, they do not require a second firing.

Gold and Silver Outlines

Several companies manufacture bright gold and silver paints that can also be used for outlining your pattern. However, since most of them must be fired at a lower temperature, they should be applied in a second firing. (See Chapter Eight for more details.) These paints can be applied with a metal outlining pen.

Glassline

Glassline Pens, made by Clay Art Center, Inc., are used for outlining and shading liquid enamel on glass. They are available in assorted lead-free colors in plastic applicator bottles. The enamels may be thinned with water. An additional tip set that fits on the bottle is perfect for drawing on glass. Tips range in size and are placed on the end of the applicator bottle to achieve a variety of line widths.

Glassline may be applied between multiple layers of glass or on the top surface for a complex multidimensional look. Glassline is compatible with most types of fusible glass and float glass. It is also compatible with other enamel paints. Glassline is best fired to 1500°F but may be fired lower or higher, depending on the results you wish to achieve.

Glassline pens come in a variety of colors and can be used for outlining or drawing on glass.

STEPS BEFORE FIRING

When you have finished painting your design, allow it to dry. Place painted side up on the prepared mold or kiln shelf. If you are using a mold, be sure to center the glass on the mold. You can laminate the paints with a second piece of glass if you prefer.

These sample tiles were hand-painted with enamels in a workshop. I am grateful to my students who gave me the opportunity to use them. Photos courtesy of Lighthouse Stained Glass, Venice, CA.

These 4" tiles were created using both liquid and dry enamels.

MORE ABOUT PAINTING

To learn more about brushes and painting, see Chapter Six. Some of you may find this material of particular interest because it describes in detail brush shapes and their capabilities. This is special information that you may not have come across elsewhere.

This panel was painted with Fuse Master powders.

The pieces shown here were painted with liquid enamels and sifted with enamel powders for additional effects.

Brush Types and Strokes

ABOUT BRUSHES

Brushes are the traditional tools for applying paint. If you are inexperienced with paint brushes, it may be awkward to produce specific strokes. With practice, however, you'll gain the confidence that will help give your work a professional look.

Choosing the right tool for a painting job is often the key to a successful painting project. Although brushes may be similar, each is capable of producing different effects. Their specific differences make each brush shape uniquely suited for a particular task.

The following descriptions should give you an idea of the many types of brushes and their uses. Various brush shapes and sizes can complement your strengths and abilities and help you to achieve details you may have thought that only an experienced artist could accomplish. Choose the shape and size of brushes to suit your painting style, your subject matter, your level of skill, and the glass you are using.

From left to right: Miracle Wedge® brush, stipple brush, ultra-round brush, angular shader brush, spotter brush, liner brush, filbert brush, wash brush, fan brush, script liner brush, and dagger striper brush. Brushes by Loew-Cornell, Inc.

BRUSH COMPOSITION

Artist brushes can be divided by hair type into three categories: natural soft animal hair, bristle, and synthetic (manufactured) hair. Certain hair types and shapes work best for particular tasks and provide maximum performance and durability. Price often indicates quality within a type of brush hair.

Brushes combining natural and synthetic hairs are also excellent brushes. Natural hair contributes softness and absorbency, while synthetic hair maintains the original firmness of fine natural hair.

Although some artists prefer the traditional natural bristle brush for painting on glass, in recent years the newer synthetic fiber brushes can offer certain advantages: (1) they are usually less expensive for comparable quality; (2) the synthetic filament is less likely to become damaged from solvents or paint; and (3) the synthetic brushes are easier to clean.

BRUSH LENGTHS AND SIZES

Manufacturers provide artists with two lengths of brush handles. Short-handled brushes are the best choice for applying paint while working on a table or slightly slanted surface.

If you are planning to paint small projects, purchase brushes with smaller bristles. Medium sizes are better for larger projects such as panels or platters.

Kay Bain Weiner

The painting was created using Unique Glass Colors with various brush shapes, enabling the artist to portray the bird, leaves, and flowers.

The flowers were painted using fine enamel powders mixed with an oil-based medium. An angular shader brush was used to create the flower petals.

BRUSHES FOR GLASS

For a wide assortment of brushes, visit your art or craft shop. The names and size numbers are displayed on the brush handles. In this section, reference is made to Loew-Cornell brushes because of their distinctive features. Their Taklon synthetic brushes are ideal for painting on hard surfaces such as glass. Many of these brushes are described in this chapter. Some of the illustrations are also courtesy of Loew-Cornell.

BRUSH SHAPES

Brushes are classified as flats or rounds, based on the shape of the ferrule where the brush hair emerges. Instructions will often refer to working a flat brush either on its "flat" or on its "chisel edge." The flat is the broad area on either side of the brush; the chisel edge refers to the thin painting surface formed by the tips of the hairs.

LOADING THE BRUSH

How you load your brush may depend on the effect you wish to achieve and the type of brush you are using. The usual recommendation is to load your brush "almost to the ferrule."

First moisten your brush. Dry bristles will absorb moisture from the paint and prevent you from achieving long, smooth, flowing strokes. Load by pulling paint from the edge of your paint puddle. ("Dipping" your brush into the center will eventually cause the bristles to flare or fan.) After pulling paint onto your brush, start with straight strokes in the same spot on your palette to work the paint evenly into your brush. When you have finished loading one side, turn your brush over and load the other side in the same manner.

FLAT BRUSHES

Hold a flat brush as you would hold a pencil: Gently grasp the handle down near the ferrule between your thumb and middle finger, with the index finger resting on top. Movement should come from your shoulder, except when executing small strokes or painting small areas where only wrist control is possible.

Shader Brush

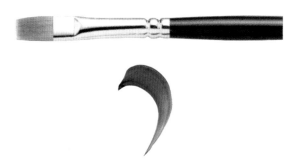

Practice making the comma stroke with different brushes to see the effect each brush shape makes.

Wash Brush

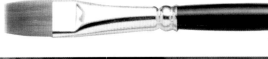

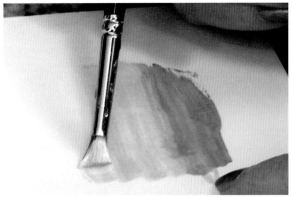

This wash brush has been double-loaded with two colors of enamel paint.

One-stroke Brush

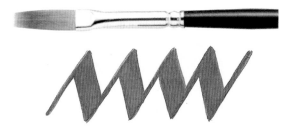

Shader Brush

This brush can be double-loaded with two colors or shades of paint. To double-load these brushes, pull each edge of your brush through a separate color and stroke the brush on one area of your palette to blend the two colors.

Wash Brush

This is a large flat brush used to create broad, sweeping strokes and washes and to apply overall base coating. Wash brushes can also be double-loaded with two colors or shades of paint.

One-stroke Brush

This brush contains extra-long hair and can hold a large amount of liquid to produce long, continuous, broad strokes without any break in continuity and coverage—essential when you are doing lettering or need long, thick lines.

Dagger Striper Brush

Load this brush as you would load a shader, with equal amounts of paint on both sides, just below the ferrule.

It is best suited for long thick-and-thin line work as in borders, vines, leaves, and ribbons. The chisel edge makes it useful for creating continuing straight or curving lines in decorative painting. Long, thick lines can be achieved without reloading when using the sword-shaped chisel edge. To achieve thin line striping, practice keeping the brush perpendicular to the surface, and use the chisel edge to pull straight lines.

As you become more comfortable with the brush, curve your lines in different directions. Hold the brush as you would hold a pencil, but lean it back at an angle that will give the chisel edge of the brush maximum contact with the surface.

Angular Shader Brush

This shader is commonly used for "S," "C," fan, and leaf strokes, and for creating leaves, roses, and rosebuds. Much like other flat brushes, this brush can be loaded with two colors of paint. Its angled shape is best suited for painting or blending in small areas and for use in corners. The "S" stroke is a thick-and-thin line created with changes in pressure. Starting on the tip, gradually add pressure as you begin the first curve in the "S," and release as you come through the second curve.

Rake Brush

When using rake brushes, it is important to find just the right balance of water and paint. Too little water will make the brush drag. Too much water will cause your lines to merge. As a general rule, you will want to use more water than you would put in a shader, but less than you would put in a liner. After loading the brush, press it down on your palette. Holding the handle vertically, twist slightly in both directions.

Dagger Striper Brush

Angular Shader Brush

Rake Brush

This will help distribute the paint and keep the brush in its rake shape.

For the most part, you will want to work with the third of the brush nearest the tip. The harder you press, the more solid color you will create. Be careful not to overload your brush.

When wet, the thin brush tip makes the hairs finger into little groups, creating a rake-like appearance. The rake is a texturizing brush. Its "S" shape is best used for quick cross-hatching and for suggesting hair, fur, wood graining, grasses, feathers, etc. The rake creates a dry brush effect. Longer strokes are used for duplicating wood texture; for adding motion and ripples to ponds, waterfalls, or waves; and for creating shadows and highlights, as on a dirt path or a barn roof.

Fan Brush

Fan Brush

The fan brush is used to create texturized grasses, shrubbery, and trees. Load the dry brush tips with paint and brush away from you. The fan is also useful for smoothing brush stroke marks.

For short, blunt grass, load just the ends of the brush with small amounts of water and paint. Push down on the flat of the brush with a short, dabbing motion. To make longer grass, load the same way, touch the ends of the brush to your painting surface, and flick the brush away from you, releasing pressure as you pull through each stroke.

For leaf-bearing trees, paint in the trunk and branches, then load the ends of your fan brush. Remove any excess paint on a paper towel. Dab lightly on and around the tree branches to obtain a light, airy look—perfect for late fall and spring trees—or continue to build up a density of color.

For palm trees, apply paint only on the ends of the brush, and work with a short, quick, dabbing motion. This will help keep the fronds of the tree from becoming too wide.

ROUND BRUSHES

When using a round brush, move your entire arm. Use your little finger as a balance to maintain the brush in a perpendicular position. Allow your arm to glide your brush and your finger fluidly around the surface.

Work from the edge of your paint puddle and pull the color out, stroking the brush on your palette in one direction. Rotate your brush, pull more paint from the edge of your puddle, and stroke the brush on your palette to work the paint up to the ferrule. Continue until the brush is evenly loaded.

Ultra-round Brush
With this brush, you can do continuous straight line work, scrolling, and calligraphy. For best results, use as a liner and keep thin paint on the tip of the brush. The ultra-round's belly acts as a reservoir, allowing continuous use without frequent reloading. To vary line thickness, slight pressure can be used. It is ideal for outlining designs.

Liner Brush
The liner produces continuous curved or straight lines of the same thickness when equal pressure is used. Thin to thick lines can be created by varying the pressure. This brush is important for monogramming,

Two colors of paint can be mixed on the glass. Use a round brush to puddle on the colors. Photo courtesy of Unique Glass Colors.

Ultra-round Brush

Liner Brush

Filbert Brush

Miracle Wedge® Brush

Spotter Brush

highlighting, and outlining. For more efficient use of the brush, thin the paint to an ink-like consistency.

Filbert Brush
The rounded shape of this brush is best used to create soft edges, to blend colors (as on a bird's breast), or to fill in areas. Its rounded tip provides a natural shape for many flower petals, leaves, and bird feathers. The flower petals in the photo on the left were created with one stroke of the filbert brush.

Miracle Wedge® Brush
The Miracle Wedge® can be loaded on three sides with different colors. Varying the pressure and the angle of placement on the surface can create multicolored effects. This brush is best used for ribbons, borders, leaves, flowers, etc. It is not one of the basic brushes but can be a handy accessory.

Spotter Brush
Use this brush for very fine details, such as intricate stroke work, eyes and eyelashes, dots, and signatures.

Tight Spot Detailer Brush
The detailer resembles a spotter with a bent handle that allows the painter easier maneuverability. The angle of this brush is such that the painter's hand is no longer directly over the painting surface.

Stippler Brushes

There are various stippler brushes. Do not wet a stippler before loading it with paint. When changing colors, cloth-wipe the paint off and be sure to allow the brush to dry partially. Load your brush by dipping just the tips in your paint and dab on your palette or a paper towel to remove the excess. Hold the brush upright. Use quick, short, up-and-down pouncing motions to tap the paint out of your brush and onto the surface.

Deerfoot Stippler Brush

Most stipplers are texturizing brushes. The hairs of the Deerfoot stippler are positioned on an angle, and when the brush is pressed to a surface, the impression looks like a deer's hoof. Hold your brush as you would hold a pencil, shortest length hairs toward you, so that all of the bristles can make contact with your painting surface.

The purpose of stippling is to create a light, airy, or fuzzy impression, and the Deerfoot stippler is terrific for creating fur, shrubbery, and leafy trees. Use with a dry brush and pouncing technique. To speckle (stipple) a piece, load the stippler with thin paint.

Tight Spot Detailer Brush

Stippler Brush

Deerfoot Stippler Brush

BRUSH CARE

1. Some general supplies to have on hand are scrap glass or a foam plate to use as a palette, a brush basin, a brush cleaner, and a mixture of vinegar and water.

2. When loading, using, or cleaning brushes, allow the hairs to move in their natural direction. Excessive pressure, twisting, or other motion can quickly cause permanent damage to a brush.

3. After submerging a brush in water, with the brush full, snap the excess water out. A quality brush will snap to an even shape and point. A brush of lesser quality will appear uneven in shape and may or may not come to a fine point.

4. Never let paint dry on a brush. Always keep brushes moist while working until proper cleaning is possible.

5. Do not mix paint with your brush. Use a palette knife on a piece of glass, on a Styrofoam plate, or on palette paper.

6. It is essential that brushes be properly and thoroughly cleaned at the end of each working session. You can clean your brushes with a commercial cleaning solution. Detergent and water will also serve the purpose. Remove any excess paint by wiping the brush gently across a paper towel, newspaper, or cloth.

7. Never leave a brush soaking in water or in a cleaning solution or other solvent for an extended period of time.

8. Remove extra moisture and reshape the head with your fingers. Cleaner or soap can be left in a synthetic brush to help maintain its shape. Rinse your brush before using it again for painting.

9. When storing brushes, make sure to either lay them flat or store them upright on their handles to eliminate any pressure on the hairs. Keep brushes covered or in a cabinet.

LEARN HOW

Now that you have read about brush shapes, sizes, and strokes, you may want to practice using the brushes seen in the illustrations. You can purchase some inexpensive water-based block printing inks or acrylics in black, white, and the three primary colors (yellow, blue, and red). Use scrap glass, heavy paper, or vellum board to work on.

Good lighting is essential. A light box and / or a true day lamp are helpful.

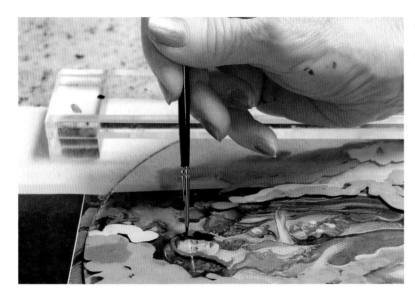

A bridge can support your hand while you are painting intricate details.

BRIDGE SUPPORT

A bridge will help support your hand while you are painting details. It is usually a strip of acrylic or wood approximately 15″ long by 1-1/2″ high and 1-1/2″ wide.

With the bridge placed parallel to your working arm and to the right of the area being painted, begin to trace your strokes. If you are left-handed, reverse the position of the bridge.

The heel of your hand should be on the bridge. The brush should be held perpendicular to the bridge and the strokes executed using a wrist or forearm movement, depending on the shape or length of the pattern.

For short strokes, your fingers will do most of the work; for longer ones, your arm will move as your hand slides along the bridge.

CHAPTER SEVEN

Unique Enamel Paint Applications

INNOVATIVE TECHNIQUES

Finding the path to any creative process involves constantly exploring the possibilities. Allow yourself to be led down many creative paths. Try combining some of the unique application techniques discussed in this chapter with your own concepts.

Borrowing innovative techniques from contemporary artists who paint with watercolors and acrylics can lead to exciting methods for applying enamel designs on glass. Brushes are traditionally the instruments used for painting on surfaces. For the adventuresome, there are unusual techniques of decorating glass without using a brush. Some of these

Leslie Perlis

Multimedia techniques applied to unusual subjects are the inspirational work of this artist. Fusible glass, powders, frit, paints, and stamped enamels are cleverly combined.

Unusual implements such as the ones pictured here can create special effects when applying enamel paints. Clockwise, from left: Rollagraph, stamp, wall texturizer, brayer.

techniques have been used on canvas, watercolor paper, walls, fabric, and other materials for years. These imaginative application methods work well with fire-on and nonfire glass paints.

Some of the ideas can be used for background textures or special design effects suitable for large or small glass concepts. A second application of paint or sifted enamels can be applied over a fired glass piece; then the decorated piece can be re-fired a second or even a third time, using any of the techniques described in this chapter. Many glass artists achieve special effects by using this method.

To experiment economically with some of these paint techniques and applications, use a piece of scrap glass and some inexpensive paint, such as water-based acrylics, block paint, or tempera.

Many of the decorating tools discussed below are surprisingly simple, yet they can create very dramatic effects. Hopefully you will be inspired to explore some of these ideas and open up artistic possibilities that you might not have otherwise conceived.

SPONGES

There are two categories of sponges—natural sea sponges and man-made synthetic.

These sponges, as well as sponge stamps, are available in art and craft stores at a reasonable price. They offer good design potential for textures, borders, and washes when used with wet enamel paints.

Sea Sponges

Natural sea sponges are available in different shapes, densities, and sizes. You can create anything from airy, textured to solid images. Sea sponges work particularly well for suggesting foliage, sea foam, or sand. For a soft, pebbled effect, sea sponges can be used to apply and blend enamel paints.

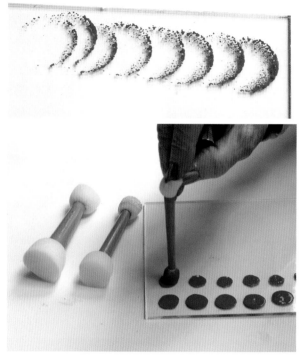

Soft sponge stamps can create all sorts of circular designs.

A sea sponge used as a stamp with two colors of paint created the border design on the glass. Natural sea sponges come in many unique shapes, enabling you to produce a variety of interesting painted patterns. The center design was produced using a wall texturizing tool.

Craft stamps are produced from rubber or from compressed sponge in an assortment of sizes.

Circular sponge stamps can create a variety of impressions on glass.

Synthetic Sponges

A compressed synthetic sponge can be cut into patterns such as stars, hearts, or letters and used as a stamp. Commercial sponge brushes can also be used to apply a wash or a design. Cellulose sponges make uniform, repetitive imprints.

You can achieve different impressions according to the way you add paint to a sponge, how you hold the sponge, and how hard you press.

Dry sponging produces dramatic effects when paint is sponged onto dry previously painted, sponged, or rubber-stamped areas.

One type of synthetic sponge, the hydrophilic sponge, does not become stiff after drying; it remains pliable and soft. Hydrophilic sponges can be found in the paint, wallpaper, and tile departments of home improvement warehouses.

Explore the Possibilities

• Add two or three other colors to the original palette or on top of one another for richer color effects.

• Sponge a design onto colored backgrounds.

• Sponge a design onto a wet surface, or wet your sponge before dipping it into the paint.

Sponging over a Grid

Lay a grid or another interesting template on your painting surface. Apply paint to the palette. Dip a sponge into the paint. Pat the excess paint onto a paper towel, and apply the paint through the grid openings with the sponge.

Besides a grid, you can find other items to use to create interesting patterns.

STAMPS

In recent years, decorative stamping has become a very popular hobby. As a result, there is a wide assortment of stamp designs available, ranging from the abstract to realistic representations of animals, plants, etc. The best stamps to use on glass are simple rubber or compressed designs that are raised and deeply incised. Avoid small intricate stamp designs because the paint tends to blur on glass.

Apply enamel paint onto the raised stamp design with a brush, and then press the stamp onto scrap glass to test, since glass will react differently than paper. Reapply paint to the stamp each time you repeat the design. After using paint on your stamps, be careful to clean them immediately with a brush and water.

Noncolored Ink Pad

For another simple stamp idea, use a blank noncolored ink pad. Soak with a medium such as Klyr Fire or Holding Medium. Press a stamp into the pad to coat with the medium, and then press the stamp onto the glass. Sift enamel powders onto the stamped area. Tip the glass to remove the excess enamel.

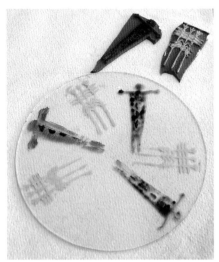

Exotic rubber stamps such as these can add decorative designs on glass dinnerware or on borders for lamp panels or boxes.

Rubber Rollagraph

Rubber rollagraph stamp wheels are available in some craft shops. They are great for border designs because they roll a continuous pattern. There is a wide selection of different pattern wheels available for purchase separately from the handle.

BRAYERS

The paint applicators called "brayers" are fun to use to apply paint to a surface. They are available at craft and hobby stores in many shapes, widths, and sizes. Some brayers can be purchased with interesting patterns and textures.

Another suggestion: Wrap a rubber or sponge brayer with one or two rubber bands. Roll the brayer into the enamel paint; then roll the brayer onto the glass to achieve a linear pattern.

PAINT AND SIFT

Apply paint to the glass and vary the background. When the surface is dry, put lace over it, and sift color over the lace.

COMB OR TEXTURIZING TOOL

Narrow lines or stripes can be created in enamels as you drag the teeth of a comb or a texturizing tool through semi-dry painted enamel. Remove some of the enamel to reveal the glass. For added interest, sift a layer of contrasting enamel powder, and then comb the surface again.

CARDBOARD STAMP

There are two different methods of working with corrugated cardboard.

One way is to apply enamel paints to a piece of ribbed-sided corrugated cardboard and use it as you would a stamp to create a linear pattern. For ease of handling, glue a dry sponge to the back of the piece of cardboard.

A second method is to cut a 2" strip of corrugated cardboard, roll it up, and secure the bundle with tape. Then hold one end of the cardboard and apply liquid enamels with a brush to the other end. Use it like a stamp by pressing the roll design onto the glass.

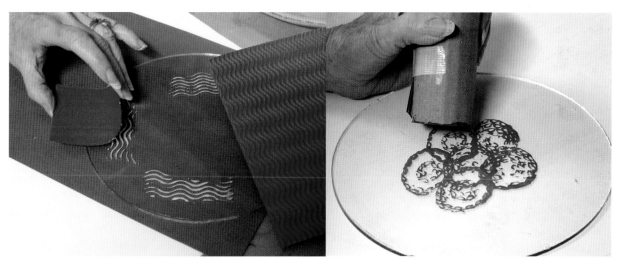

A linear design can be accomplished by stamping the glass with a piece of corrugated cardboard.

A strip of corrugated cardboard was rolled and taped together to create a stamp. One end is painted with liquid enamels and stamped on the glass to create the design.

This surf scene (right) was created by painting enamels onto aluminum foil. Painted foil was placed on the clear glass (below). A brayer was then rolled over the back of the foil. The foil was lifted, leaving an impression of the surf. After the paint dried, seagulls and surfers were loosely drawn using a spotter brush. Demonstration by Kay Bain Weiner.

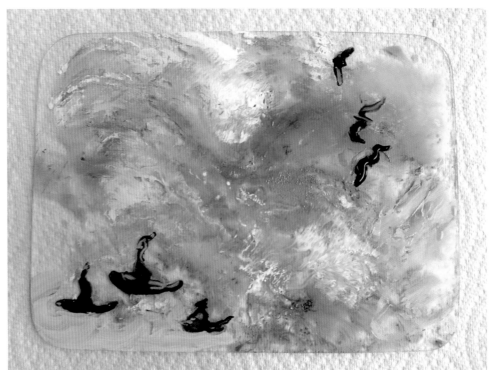

Several feet of twine bunched up into a ball can be used to apply paint and impress distinctive texture.

SGRAFFITO

Sgraffito is a decorating approach that takes its name from the Italian word for "scratch." For an interesting effect, apply a heavy coat of paint to the glass using several colors. Allow the paint to dry. With an eraser, stylus, comb, or other appropriate implement, remove some of the paint to reveal the glass. This technique can also be achieved by first sifting powder instead of painting.

TWINE OR STRING

To create a distinctive pattern, use a ball of twine or string. Roll the ball into wet enamel paint and use it like a stamp to apply a design to the glass surface.

For an irregular pattern, unravel the ball of string and rewind it unevenly. Apply enamel paint and press the ball onto the surface for a different pattern, such as irregular dots, lines, or textures.

REVERSE MONOPRINT

With a brush or painting knife, paint a shiny finished paper, such as wax paper or aluminum foil, with a pattern or design. Press the glass on top of the painted design while it is still wet. (See previous page.)

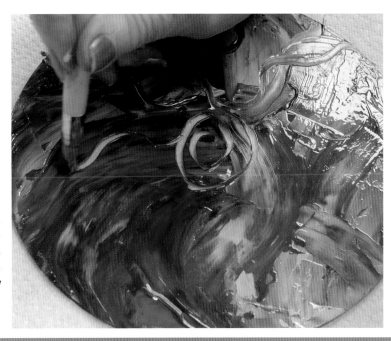

Using a sgraffito technique, a colorfully painted glass disk is enhanced using a tool to remove some of the wet paint. The glass will be fired over a drape mold to become a free form vase. Demonstration by Kay Bain Weiner.

APPLICATOR-TIPPED BOTTLES

Use squeeze bottles with small metal applicator tips to apply wet enamels and create unusual designs. You can find small squeeze bottles with various sized metal tips in craft stores. The bottles can be filled using an extruder (a large plastic syringe),.

CREDIT CARDS AND PAINT SCRAPERS

Even credit cards or a variety of paint scrapers may be used to apply enamel paint to produce patterns. Paint the edge of the card or paint scraper to apply linear geometric designs.

Enamel paint can be applied to the edge of an old credit card. Use the card as a stamp to create a linear design.

Impressions of Monet's waterlilies were created by applying wet enamels on glass with a painting knife. When the paint was dry, several paint techniques were used to create the different textures, including sponging and applicator bottle. Dichroic frit was positioned on the glass for the lily pads. Demonstration by Kay Bain Weiner.

TEXTURIZING WITH FEATHERS

Feathers have been used by various artists to achieve unusual effects with paints. The feathers can create texture or streaks in wet paint, thus adding interest to the decorated surface. Texturizing feathers, such as those manufactured by Loew-Cornell, are available from art and craft stores.

To create a marble effect, the artist used the light touch of a "painting" feather to pull across the soft paint.

Gold mica powder was mixed with Fuse Master Water Friendly Medium. To create gold veins in the marble tile, the tip of the feather was dipped into the mixture.

The mica mix was applied lightly, using a feather to add streaks. The images on this page are demonstrations by Linda Scott.

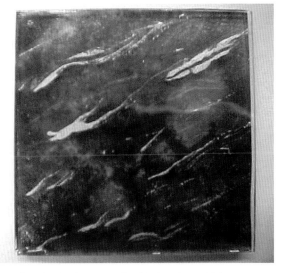

The finished tile was finally laminated by adding another layer of clean glass.

A painting knife can be used to apply enamel paints to decorate the glass.

Airbrushing is an unusual and effective method of applying enamel paints to glass.

PAINTING KNIFE

Both fine and 80-mesh enamel powders can be mixed with a water-based medium to a paste consistency. With a painting knife, spread the enamel paste onto the desired areas of the glass.

Try applying paint with a painting knife to achieve bold strokes and create an interesting style. Knife painting is a versatile and effective method of building up layers of paint. Painting knives are available in metal or plastic, in different sizes and shapes. A painting knife has a very springy, responsive blade. You can apply the paint in broad sweeps with the flat of the knife or use the tip to get sharp, angular marks. The edge of the blade makes fine linear marks. (See the finished piece on page 84.)

AIRBRUSHING GLASS

Thinned liquid enamel paints made from fine powder can be sprayed through conventional spraying equipment such as an airbrush. More consistent effects can be achieved with a larger gravity-fed spray gun, which results in a more uniform and graded finish.

LOOKING AHEAD

With some experimentation, you will come up with your own adaptations of the ideas presented in this chapter. They can lead you to develop a whole new style or technique. Whatever the results, it will be fascinating to explore the possibilities.

Additions and Inclusions for Special Effects

A VARIETY OF PRODUCTS

There are a number of products that can be used to enhance your enamel art, including decals; luster powders; sheet copper foil; mica flakes; gold, silver, and copper leaf; and metal wire.

Pat Diacca Topp

This plate is a good example of the effectiveness of using decals over fired enamels. Several decal patterns were fired onto this fused plate. Most decals must be fired at a lower temperature (1250°F); therefore, this is usually done as the last firing.

Pat Diacca Topp

Overlays of decals fired on this enamel plate enhance the geometric pattern.

LUSTER AND PATTERN DECALS

Give your fired piece additional interest and depth by applying solid luster or pattern decals. Decal material has some very unique characteristics, being both reflective and transparent to some extent. Various types of luster and pattern sheets are available from hot glass suppliers.

Carefree Luster™ Decals

Carefree Lusters™, with a metallic shimmer, are mica-based luster pigments stabilized on a paper backing for glass. Lusters are available in several solid colors on decal sheets. Both Carefree Lusters™ and pattern decals manufactured by Thompson Enamel usually mature at a lower temperature than some enamels—1250°F to 1300°F. They should therefore be fired onto a pre-fused piece.

Pattern Decals

These decals come in an array of patterns that can be cut easily with regular scissors or craft pattern scissors into strips of designs. Craft paper punches are available in numerous patterns such as stars, hearts, florals, etc., and work well to cut out designs. You can use the negative or positive design to fire on your fused enamel piece.

How To Use Decals

1. In a plastic or glass container, add room-temperature water (preferably distilled). Place one cut-out decal into the water with the paper side up (luster or pattern side down to prevent excess curling). Leave for 30 to 60 seconds, depending on the size of the decal.

2. The decal should start to slip quite easily from the backing paper. If you are working with very small pieces, you may wish to use a pair of fine tweezers. Place the decal on the fired decorated glass.

3. Using a soft tissue or paper towel dampened slightly with water, hold the decal in place with the paper on top so the decal doesn't stick to your fingers. Gently wipe off excess luster or gelatin. Don't worry if some of the luster has leaked from beneath the decal; it will not affect the firing.

4. Allow each decal to dry before applying additional ones. When all decals are dry, fire the glass to 1250°F.

The ProFusion Company also manufactures decal sheets that have good pattern designs. ProFusion decals can be fired at a temperature range from 1450°F to 1550°F. Use the above directions to apply these decals to glass.

Craft paper punches are available in numerous designs. They can be used to cut out decals or sheet copper foil. The punches can also be used to create cardboard stencil designs through which to paint or sift enamels.

Craft paper border punches with intricate designs can be used for cutting out decals or sheet copper to be used along a border.

SHEET COPPER

A small quantity of sheet copper can be laminated between two layers of glass. For instance, if you are creating a floral design with enamels, you can add copper leaves. Use thin .002-gauge sheet copper without adhesive.

Limit the amount of copper to be fired between the glass sheets to no more than 20 percent of the size of the glass. Do not place the copper near the edges, or the layers of glass will not fuse together properly. The copper will change to a reddish-brown color during firing. The cleaner and less oxidized the copper inclusion, the brighter the color will be.

To emboss the copper, place the sheet copper over a soft pad—a computer pad or a magazine, for example. Place the pattern over the copper, trace it with a pen, and draw in any linear details. Cut out the traced copper pattern with scissors. Craft punches can also be used to cut out unique designs in the copper.

MICA POWDERS AND FLAKES

Mica particles appear to be metallic, yet they are actually a mineral and are available in several colors and sizes. These sparkling powders or flakes can be sprinkled on decorated glass and laminated between the glass layers. The fine mica powders can also be applied to a single or top piece

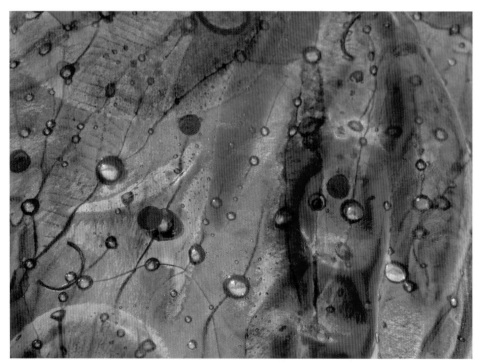

Janet Zambai

The artist airbrushed glass with Reusche transparent low fire paints. She also included sheet copper cut into medallions between layers of glass.

of glass after first spraying or painting a medium on the desired glass area.

LIQUID GOLD AND SILVER PAINT

Gold and silver paint (oil-based) is available to enhance dishes, jewelry, and all other enamel art. It is costly and is packaged in small bottles. However, it adds a shiny, elegant touch. It has a tendency to thicken in the bottle over time, but it can be thinned down with the manufacturer's solvent. Most of these paints must be applied to pre-fired enamel pieces because they need to be fired at a lower temperature than the enamels, between approximately 1200°F and 1300°F.

The metallics are true solutions of precious metals in solvents and oils. When applied, these solutions normally appear oily brown; but once fired, they reveal brilliant metallic tones. Because of the risk of contamination, you should not work from the original container, but transfer the amount needed to another container, to a palette, or into an outlining pen.

Applying Metallics

When applying metallics, a brush, sponge, stamp, outlining pen, or other method may be employed. Special effects can be obtained by using a mixture of colors. Experiment with firing techniques, such as varying the firing temperature or doing multiple firings of an individual piece.

Using an Outlining Pen

1. Fill the outlining pen with a drop of liquid metallic and complete pattern outlines.

2. Clean pen with lacquer thinner.

3. Allow outlines to dry.

4. Fire between 1200°F and 1300°F.

This glass pendant was first fully fused. An outlining pen was used to apply the liquid gold paint in a linear pattern on top. The pendent was then fired to 1250°F.

METAL WIRE

Various types of metal wire can be laminated between two layers of glass. Thin gauges (between 24- and 12-gauge) of nichrome, silver, copper tinned, copper, or brass wire can be fired successfully between layers of glass.

This capability is especially helpful to glass artists who create jewelry; they can fuse the jumplinks needed to attach earring wires or pendants. Some commercial wire jewelry findings, such as eye pins and jumplinks can also be successfully laminated between glass. See Chapter Eleven for information on laminating metals.

GOLD, SILVER, AND COPPER LEAF

Wafer thin sheets of precious metals (22-karat gold, pure silver, and copper), often used in refurbishing antiques, are readily available in leaf form and can be used for special effects between layers of glass and enamel. They can also be applied to a top layer of glass by adhering the metal to brushed-on liquid medium. Gold and

Carmen Reynolds

Thin copper leaf can be laminated between layers of glass for added special effects and sparkle, as shown in this plate.

silver leaf is readily available in very thin foil (85.7 mm x 85.7 mm). It can be handled more conveniently with tweezers. It is often used by fusers of glass jewelry or for borders around plates or accents in tiles. Both gold and silver leaf also come in a slightly thicker foil (Bullseye Glass Co.) that is easier to handle.

TIP TOP-IC

When firing your project with the inclusion of sheet copper or gold or silver leaf foil, start heating the glass slowly. Refer to Chapter Eleven.

GLUES AND ADHESIVES

Glues are generally not used in glass enameling, but there are specialty glues manufactured for the glass artist. For example, when you are working with glass enamels, you might want to embellish the design with glass stringers and noodles, larger frit, or pieces of glass, all of which can be held temporary in place with glue or adhesive.

DICHROIC GLASS

Dichroic sheet glass and frit give the artist another medium for self-expression.

Dichroic glass appears to be comprised of several colors; however, it is transmitted color that reflects different hues, depending on what angle you look at it.

Dichroic fusible frit, unlike other frit, is produced by coating small pieces of glass. Therefore, you can crush the dichroic frit even smaller and still get the dichroic effect. Dichroic frit can be used as accent highlights in an enamel project.

MISCELLANEOUS MATERIAL

Unique items that can be laminated for special effects between layers of fusible glass include strands of fiberglass, mother-of-pearl, leaves, cellophane wrappers, and fine luster powders.

Howard Sandberg

The bowl was fused with dichroic glass. Then dichroic frit was texture-fired to give a sparkle finish.

FINE LUSTER POWDERS

Available in several colors, these shimmering powders can add depth and beauty to your enamel art.

Luster powders are best laminated between glass. However, they can also be applied by brushing on a medium first and sifting the powders on top.

Because these powders can easily become airborne, wearing a mask is recommended when you are working with them.

BUBBLES

You may want to intentionally create a bubble in a particular area of a laminated project—to define, for example, the eye of a fish. Mix a teaspoon of clothing detergent with a few drops of water. Wipe away the enamel in the area you want the bubble to appear. Apply a small dot of the paste mixture between two pieces of glass before firing.

Dan Fenton

A black glass background and sifted enamel powders (by Thompson Enamel) were used to create this plate. The figure is highlighted with iridescent and bright metallic lusters. Fusing and slumping were accomplished in one firing. The artist obtained the figures from computer clip art which he redesigned to create hand-made stencils. Photo courtesy of Scott Emslie of Sunshine Glass.

CHAPTER NINE

Color Selection

THE IMPORTANCE OF COLOR

If you are a beginner working with enamels, you may not be concerned with color relationships. However, as you gain experience, knowing more about color will enable you to create more sophisticated works of art. It will also help you to mix enamel colors successfully.

A little knowledge regarding color relationships can aid you in selecting harmonious and dynamic color combinations. Your designs will be enhanced by color choices whether your work is contemporary, abstract, whimsical, or traditional.

If you paint, weave, or produce glass art, colors can have a tremendous impact. It is important to select colors wisely. Shading can add realism and depth to objects. A fish, a bird, or a flower will appear flat unless warms and cools, darks and lights, are used to suggest dimensions.

Leslie Perlis

Bold complementary colors are used in this sink backsplash. The artist employs a combination of stamped enamels, glass powder, and frit.

WARM COLORS/COOL COLORS

Generally speaking, hues on the red side of the color spectrum are the warm, more stimulating colors; those on the blue side are the cool, calmer colors.

Warm colors (reds, yellows, whites, oranges, golds) tend to come forward and appear closer and larger, while cool colors (blues, greens, violets, grays, silvers) recede or appear to be farther away. Warm and cool color combinations can create perspective. If you take advantage of this fact, you can produce more-professional-looking art objects. For instance, a bright red apple can look more realistic if you use warm tones on the front of the apple and make the sides darker or duller, by shading them with a darker or duller red. Light colors give the appearance of expansion, while dark colors give the illusion of contraction.

COLOR PERSPECTIVE

In nature, distant parts of the scenery—mountains, for example—look bluish. Even farther back, mountains appear to be more gray or violet; they also appear smaller and hazier.

By skillfully combining warm and cool colors, you can create the illusion of depth and achieve a more realistic visual effect.

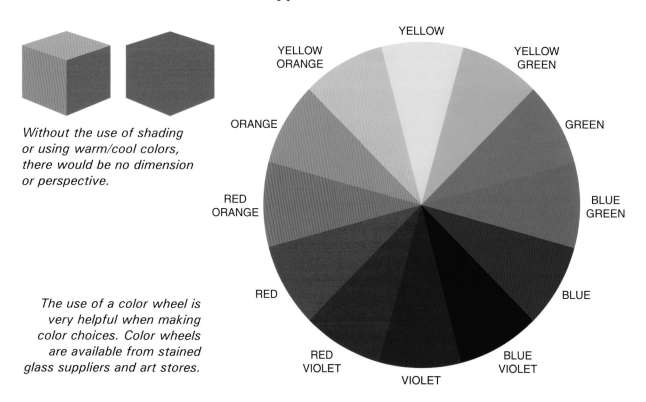

Without the use of shading or using warm/cool colors, there would be no dimension or perspective.

The use of a color wheel is very helpful when making color choices. Color wheels are available from stained glass suppliers and art stores.

YELLOW

YELLOW
ORANGE

YELLOW
GREEN

ORANGE

GREEN

RED
ORANGE

BLUE
GREEN

RED

BLUE

RED
VIOLET

BLUE
VIOLET

VIOLET

Robert Leatherbarrow

A primary color scheme is used to create this unique art piece. Six layers of base glass, colored powders, and frit were fired in four separate kiln firings. The artist says, "By mixing frit and powders, it is possible to grade and shade colors, and create interesting vein-like textures."

Weave the warm colors through the cools to create more dynamic color combinations.

COLOR WHEEL

The basic color wheel consists of three primary, three secondary, and six tertiary colors.

Primary Colors
The primary colors are red, yellow, and blue.

Secondary Colors
The secondary colors are orange, green, and purple. It takes two primary colors to create these colors, so you can create some of your own shades.

When using opaque enamel powders, the individual dry opaque enamel particles do not actually change color when mixed; they only appear to do so. For instance, when using blue and yellow together, we only perceive green. This is referred to as the "Bezold effect."

With the three primary and three secondary colors, plus black and white, a painter can mix any color of enamel that a project demands.

Tertiary Colors
The mix of one primary color and one secondary color creates a tertiary color such as yellow-green.

Margot Clark

This enamel plate incorporates a warm analogous color scheme on a cool background. On a dark background, warm, light colors appear more intense.

Complementary Colors

Complementary colors are hues opposite each other on the color wheel, such as red and green, yellow and violet, orange and blue.

When two complementary colors are placed side by side, each color seems more intense than if it were by itself. A small patch of red in a large area of green (complementary colors) can make both the red and the green look much brighter. The visual impact of complementary colors is significant; by controlling them carefully in your art, you can achieve dramatic results.

The color of a beach in the evening could be effectively suggested by using a purple shadow (cool color) on the yellow beach (warm color). The violet/yellow complement combination makes both colors more luminous.

You can create an optical illusion by using a complementary color scheme. Complementary colors placed side by side in equal proportions in equal intensities and value appear to vibrate. This is a phenomenon that can be put to exciting use in art.

Analogous Colors

Analogous colors are hues that are adjacent on the color wheel, such as red, orange, and yellow, or green, blue, and violet, and all shades in between. Analogous color schemes present visually harmonious color combinations.

Monochromatic Colors

Several values (lighter or darker) or tones of one color are called "monochromatic colors." A color scheme based on monochromatic colors is usually very appealing.

Dominant Color

Whatever your color scheme, you should select only one dominant color, allowing this color to set the tone for the entire color scheme. The other colors used should be less striking in either saturation or value.

COLOR ILLUSIONS

Colors are influenced in hue by adjacent colors, each tinting its neighbor with the complement. Make one hue more dominant and the other less intense, or smaller in area, or varied in tone. You can create a dynamic effect by using a small amount of a complementary color as a sharp accent. For instance, the colors become more vibrant when you highlight a monochromatic scheme, such as blue, with a touch of its complementary color, orange.

Color Intensity

Color intensity (luminosity) is altered according to the color of the background. On a white background, light colors decrease in intensity, whereas on a black background, light colors increase in intensity. (See photo below.)

Color Relationships

Colors do not work in isolation. For example, a tone that appears dark on its own will appear much lighter when surrounded by darker tones. Similarly, a warm color may appear quite cool when surrounded by even warmer colors.

Color Facts

Colors change with light source and lighting conditions. As glass artists, we are aware of the color change that occurs in glass as the time of day changes. Warm colors have long wave lengths, and cool colors have short wave lengths. As twilight progresses, some of the long wave lengths are lost, and the short wave lengths become dominant. Therefore, a bright red becomes darker as twilight changes into evening, and cool colors appear more intense.

THE "COLOR" OF WHITE

Although white itself has no actual color, it picks up and reflects colors from its surroundings. Therefore it is almost never really white, but a composite of other colors. White snow, for example, may appear yellowish on a sunny day; yet on a cloudy day, it may appear blue or violet because it reflects the sky.

If you are using white to paint flowers, for instance, the white petals should have shading either near the edges or in the center, to appear more realistic. You can break up stark white with a hint of other hues. This will give your white a vibrant quality. (See photo on page 102.)

Steve Maddy

These colorful plates and trays were created with low fire enamel stains. The vibrant warm colors become more intense because they are surrounded by dark hues.

Color Relationships

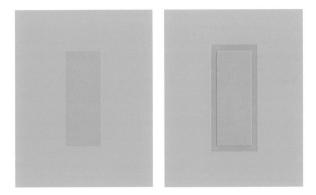  

See how much brighter the blue appears when it is surrounded by its complement, orange. The blue next to the green seems pale and weak.

Dark hues on a noncomplementary background (such as royal blue on purple), will appear weaker than on a complementary background (such as royal blue on red).

Note that green against yellow looks both smaller and darker in value, while green against blue looks larger and takes on a yellow cast.

Dark hues, such as purple, red, etc., appear stronger if surrounded by light complementary colors or narrow bands of white.

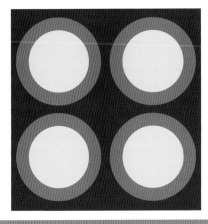 

Far Left: When a warm color such as red is used on a cool background, it appears to come forward. Note that the yellow seems to be even closer. The illusion of depth is evident.

Left: With the opposite use of warm and cool colors in this illustration, the color images appear flat and less dimensional.

Michael Dupille

Purchased by the Washington State Arts Commission, this profound wall panel combines fused glass, enamels, and powders to achieve a technique the artist has perfected and termed "Fritology." The white color of the bird has hints of other colors, giving the white a more vibrant quality.

The patterns of animal fur such as zebra, leopard, or giraffe are often used for design purposes, as seen in this glass enamel tile.

Inexperienced artists will often use solid white or black to depict white or black objects; but if touches of other hues are added, those areas will be more luminous.

ANIMAL PRINTS

Animal prints (zebra striping, for example) can inspire welcoming color schemes for tiles and other accessory items.

CHEMISTRY AND COLOR

The following information is paraphrased from Color Cues—a series of pamphlets researched and published by Bullseye Glass Co. For the original articles in their entirety, see www.bullseyeglass.com.

Chemical Color Changes
The chemistry that happens between glass

colors at 1500°F is never totally predictable. Test small samples of the actual glass you will use in your project. Keep these samples for later reference.

Like ceramic tile, fabric, or carpet, glass is produced in batches. And, as with these other materials, there will be slight variations from one batch to the next. Buy enough of your enamels and glass to complete a project. Some glass manufacturers date color runs. Try to purchase glass produced on the same date.

Compatibility Changes

Taking certain glasses to excessively high temperatures for extremely long periods, or reheating them multiple times, can cause their chemistry to change sufficiently to alter their compatibility. Transparent reds, yellows, and oranges are more prone to this reaction than most other glass.

Reactions Between Colors

Certain colors have unique reactions when fired in contact with one another.

Firing a glass containing sulfur adjacent to a glass containing copper, for example, will usually create copper sulfate, causing a deep-walnut-brown shade along the interface. To prevent this reaction, place a thin layer of clear glass between the two glasses you are using. Certain glass colors—reds, yellows, oranges, and gold pinks—deepen when they are preheated.

STUDYING COLOR

Look carefully at nature: the water, the sky, the animals, and other objects. Train your eye to notice their color nuances as they truly are, as opposed to what you think they should be. There are several shades of green in the shrubbery, trees, and grass, and many shades of blue and green in the sea.

As you gain confidence regarding your color choices, you will probably become more inventive. You will enjoy the process of creating, and your work will be much more sophisticated and expressive.

Molds

TYPES OF MOLDS

A wide variety of glass fusing ceramic and stainless steel molds in various sizes and shapes are available from art glass suppliers. Bowl and plate molds that are used for slumping glass are sometimes referred to as "saggers." Flower formers or molds where the glass forms over the outside are often called "drapers."

In addition to tableware shapes, molds come in the shapes of butterflies, masks, flowers, soap dishes, and a wide array of decorative accessory items. Jewelry molds are available in very petite sizes (as small as 1/2" in diameter).

CERAMIC MOLDS

Some ceramic molds are thicker and denser than others. Since there is more heat concentration in thicker, denser molds, the glass may reach the desired temperature faster than in a thinner mold. It is always wise to do a test firing with a blank piece of glass.

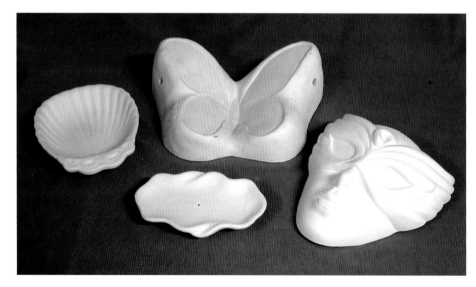

Here are a few of the interesting glass mold shapes available from art glass suppliers.

Paula Kinnman

Molds come in a wide variety of shapes and sizes. This fused glass seashell-shaped dish is embellished with liquid enamels and gold paint.

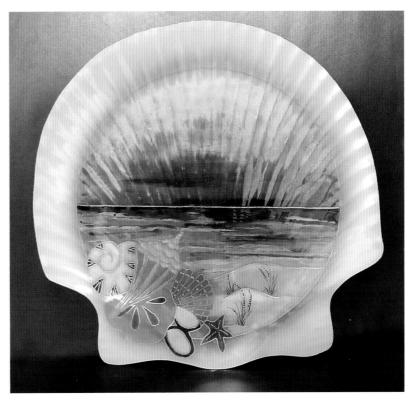

If you want to mature the enamels and form the glass in one firing, flatter molds with a gradual curve are better than deeper molds. To create bowls in a deep mold, I suggest fusing the two decorated layers of glass flat on a kiln shelf. The glass fuses and the enamels mature between 1480°F and 1550°F, depending on the glass used. Since slumping occurs at approximately 1350°F, the decorated fused glass can then be formed in the bowls for a second firing.

Greenware

Ceramic greenware (available at ceramic shops) can be used for glass molds. Greenware will become durable bisque and serviceable as a glass mold when fired between 1750°F and 1800°F. Usually a ceramic shop will fire it to bisque for you.

Plates

To create a plate using liquid or dry enamels, laminate the enamels between two layers of clear glass in the manner described earlier in this book. If you plan to use a drape mold with a single piece of glass, the enamel will be on the underside of the plate after it is fired.

Glass should be cut to the same diameter as the mold or a bit smaller, but never larger than the mold.

Jayne Persico

Colour de Verre ceramic molds enable you to produce various pate de verre glass objects. Photo courtesy of J.P. Glassworks Studio, Hazleton, PA.

PATE DE VERRE

There are ceramic molds available that enable you to produce a pate de verre glass object with ease. Glass enamels are used as the base coat to create the ornament color. The remainder of the mold is filled with clear glass frit.

TIP TOP-IC
Glass should always be placed in a sagger or on a drape mold decorated side up! The maturing temperature of the colors is hot enough to cause the glass to conform to the shape of the mold being used, so you will be decorating and forming the glass at the same time.

METAL MOLDS

Stainless steel molds are good conductors of heat. Therefore, they heat faster than molds made of thick, dense materials such as clay or ceramic.

Stainless steel molds last indefinitely. They are more suitable for draping glass on the outside—the popular flower formers, for example. Since the metal contracts more than the glass, the fired glass, when cooled, can be easily removed from the mold.

Although there is a good selection of stainless steel molds available, you might find other interesting stainless steel shapes. For instance, stainless mixing bowls can be

Gil Reynolds

Low fire enamels were painted on the glass. The decorated glass was then draped and fired over a metal flower former. Metal flower former molds are ideal for draping glass.

adapted for use as molds. If they are more than 1-1/2" deep, you will need to drill two or three small air holes in the bottom for ventilation.

STACKING

If you are working with two or three ceramic or metal plate molds of the same size and shape, you can use plate stackers (available from ceramic shops) to stack them. These can be fired only in a kiln that has side heating elements. In this case, do not use a kiln shelf so that you can stack two or three molds in layers.

Mold stackers can be used in a kiln that has side firing elements.

107

FIBER BOARD MOLDS

To help you create your own unique shape or design, either large or small, there is a product called "fiber board." Fiber board (such as Kaiser-Lee) can be carved, cut, and shaped. Fiber board comes in three thicknesses: 1", 1-1/2", and 2". The standard board is 24" x 36". Fiber board is available through glass suppliers. It offers you the opportunity to custom design and instantly create molds and use them over and over again. The board is thick and has a compact composition that enables you to easily carve an intricate bas relief design into the surface. Create molds for large bowls, picture frames, and boxes or for small accessory items such as napkin rings, drawer pulls, doorknobs, and cabinet handles.

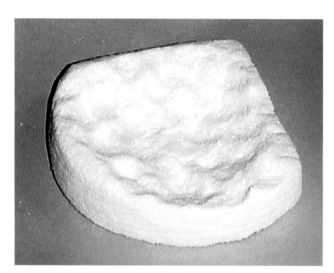

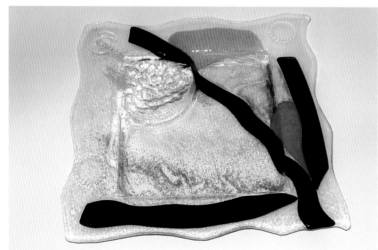

Petra Kaiser

Fiber board (Kaiser-Lee) makes an excellent mold material. The fiber board can be carved to create a texture, as seen in the first photo. A serving dish mold has been constructed using fiber board (second photo). The fused glass and enamel serving dish has conformed to the shape of the mold (third photo).

108

Your design can be drawn freehand or lightly traced with a pencil on the board. A different design can be carved on the reverse side of the board, allowing you to use the board more economically. This procedure works for pieces of jewelry or other small designs, such as three-dimensional leaves and flowers.

Since fiber board is easy to cut, carve, and shape, there is no need to purchase special or expensive tools. Cut it with a stencil cutter, kitchen knife, or putty knife. Carve designs with a spoon, a pencil, or linoleum cutting tools. You can create either slump or drape molds with ease. Molds can be constructed to cast glass as thick as 2″.

For a very smooth finished project, sand the fiber board with fine sandpaper. Sand gently, as the surface smooths very quickly.

Apply separator (kiln wash) several times, and fire the mold without the glass. This will serve to dry and smooth the mold.

Remember that fiber board is delicate. It should be handled and stored carefully. With proper care, it will last for many uses.

WET PACK OR MOIST PACK

Wet pack or moist pack refers to a refractory fiber blanket that is ideal for creating custom molds for glass bending.

TIP TOP-IC
It is important to remember when cutting fiber board, to avoid breathing dust particles. Wear a mask and goggles for protection. To avoid creating dust, fiber board may be wet before cutting. However, it must be thoroughly dry before firing. Fiber board can be dried in the kiln, or it can be air dried.

It can be purchased either presoaked or dry in rolls which you can moisten with a ridgidizer (an inorganic binding agent).

This moist blanket can be formed over an existing shape. To keep the blanket from sticking, the original shape can be coated with a release, such as liquid detergent or nonstick spray. Allow the blanket mold to air dry or sun dry. This can take three or four days. When your mold is completely dry, it can be coated with a few layers of mold resist.

Do not sand the dry mold before it has been coated because the fibers are dangerous to breathe! Coats of liquid resist painted on your mold will make it smooth.

Alumina rigidizer hardener is used for hardening and increasing the refractory properties of alumina silicate fiber products. Dry ceramic papers or blankets can also be rigidized with this hardening liquid.

MOLD COMPOUNDS

Some companies offer refractory molding compounds developed specifically for glass slumping and casting. These offer you the opportunity to create unique shapes. The directions for mixing these compounds vary and usually appear on the package.

Annette Laabs Paajanen

A sconce mold was created using a plastic sand bucket. The blue mosaic glass was slumped over the sconce mold. Photo courtesy of Best Mix Products, West Linn, OR.

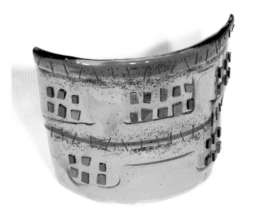

Annette Laabs Paajanen

This oval-shaped mold was created by using a plastic carrying bin. Best Mix is an easy-to-use powder mold mix with directions for use included. Photo courtesy of Best Mix Products, West Linn, OR.

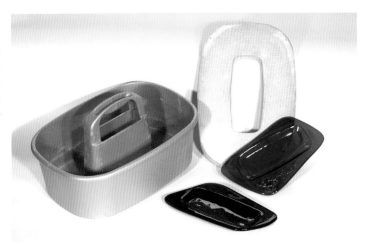

Bruce Laughlin

By making his own molds, the artist can create unusual shapes and textures. Dry enamel powders sifted on the glass give the platter its color.

CHAPTER ELEVEN

Firing Enamel Projects

GENERAL INFORMATION

Various hot glass techniques and types of glass require different firing procedures. However, the directions regarding firing in this chapter are specific for glass enameling in one firing.

To mature (fuse) enamels, laminate layers of glass, or slump glass into molds, knowledge regarding firing in a kiln is required. Medium to high fire enamels mature at a temperature range between 1350°F and 1500°F, depending on the manufacturer of the powders, frit, and glass used. Laminating layers of glass and slumping both require a firing temperature between 1475°F and 1550°F—the range where the glass and enamels become one and take the shape of the mold.

Every kiln is different, with its own heating and cooling characteristics. If you are inexperienced at operating a kiln, fire a few test pieces. It is important to keep notes on your firing schedule so that they can be used for future reference. Make and record necessary adjustments in your firing schedule based on your own observations.

FIRING PROJECTS 12″ OR UNDER

The following instructions will be helpful for painted or sifted enamel projects 12″ or under with one or two layers of glass without the use of a medium or adhesive, using a kiln with manual or digital controls. The suggested firing schedules are conservative. If you have had experience, you might want to use a different or more aggressive schedule.

> **TIP TOP-IC**
> If your kiln is new, be sure to coat the bottom and shelves (explained in Chapter Three). During first use, the kiln elements may give off smoke. Therefore, your kiln may require pre-firing. Refer to your kiln manual.

When placing the glass and mold in the kiln, leave at least 1-1/2" between the mold and the elements. Photo courtesy of Unique Glass Colors.

Manually Operated Kilns

1. Start the kiln on low with the peephole and lid closed until the pyrometer reads 500°F.

2. Turn the control dial to medium until the temperature reaches 1200°F.

3. At 1200°F, turn the control dial to high.

4. Turn the kiln off when it reaches the following temperature for your specific glass project:

- 96 COE glass—1479°F
- 90 COE glass—1500°F
- Float glass—1550°F

5. Open the kiln peephole and lid for 30 seconds to flash cool the chamber. This will stop the heating process.

6. Close the door and peephole and allow the kiln to cool naturally. You can safely peek in and check the firing process once the kiln has reached 500°F.

Firing a Kiln with Digital Controls

1. Set the program to rise 600°F per hour until the temperature reaches 1000°F.

2. At 1000°F, set the program for 300°F per hour until the pyrometer reaches the appropriate temperature for your glass, as given under "Manually Operated Kilns."

This more gradual temperature increase will help squeeze out any bubbles.

3. Set the kiln to soak for 10 minutes.

4. Allow the kiln to cool until the pyrometer reaches 300°F before attempting to remove the project.

If you've used two pieces of glass, you will know that the firing is complete when the edges have rounded and become one. The glass will appear shiny and wet when it is in the process of fusing.

For more firing information on kilns with digital controls, refer to the glass manufacturers' websites listed at the back of this book.

FIRING USING A MEDIUM

If you are using a medium or adhesive to create your project, proceed according to the following firing method. Added organic material, such as white glue, fiber paper, and binding agents, will volatilize, and the fumes will dissipate.

1. Turn the kiln on low.

2. Leave the lid slightly open and the peephole out until the pyrometer reads 500°F. Venting will allow any fumes or other gaseous materials to exit the kiln and not contaminate the surface of the glass.

3. At 500°F, close the peephole and the lid.

4. Follow steps 2 through 6 under "Manually Operated Kilns."

ANNEALING

Annealing is the process of slowing down the cooling process through the temperature range from 1000°F to 750°F to prevent internal stress within the glass. Annealing is not necessary if the enamel project is smaller than 12" or under 5/16" thick. Usually the ceramic bricks in the kiln retain heat longer than the glass. This natural cooling process usually provides adequate annealing for smaller projects.

A kiln constructed of fiber may cool too quickly; therefore annealing the glass projects will be a necessity even if the projects are under 8". Photo courtesy of Lighthouse Stained Glass, Venice, CA.

If you do not have a computerized kiln to automatically anneal your projects, wait until the kiln has cooled down to 850°F. Set the kiln control on low, maintaining the temperature between 850°F and 1000°F for one hour. Turn off the kiln and allow it to cool naturally.

Your kiln may cool down too quickly if it is constructed of fiber or is not well insulated. Once your glass has been fused and the kiln is turned off, time the cooling rate. Begin timing after the temperature has cooled to 1000°F. The temperature should not drop faster than 2°F per minute, or about 120°F per hour. If the kiln's temperature drops more than 120°F per hour, it will be necessary to anneal the project.

ENAMEL FIRING STAGES

Here is the cycle of changes that occur in glass at various temperatures:

• From 1000°F to 1300°F—The glass remains a rigid blank, although it is expanding invisibly.

• From 1300°F to 1350°F—The glass starts rounding at the edges and sags slightly. Opaque enamels begin to mature at this temperature but can be fired as high as 1550°F for float glass.

• From 1350°F to 1400°F—The glass may be completely bent, or very nearly so,

TIP TOP-IC
If you wish to remove your fired project from the kiln at 350°F, the following will be helpful: Use fireproof gloves and place the piece between two pieces of thick fiber blanket for insulation. If the project has been fired in a mold, put the glass and mold into the blanket. If time allows, leave the glass in the kiln to cool completely.

depending on its hardness and the type of kiln used.

• From 1450°F to 1550°F—Depending on the glass and kiln, the glass will be ideally laminated (and sagged if you are using a mold).

• Beyond 1550°F—Further distortion takes place. Commercial glass forms needle-like points, and any surface colorants begin to recede from the outer edge inward.

When the project is properly fired, the edges of the two pieces of glass will round and form a single layer, and the enamels and glass will glisten. If the edges of your fused piece are not rounded, then you may not have fired the piece enough. Just heat it again, this time firing it a bit higher (or soaking it a bit longer). Keep a close watch on the piece, and let it fire or soak until the edges round.

IMPORTANT FIRING TIPS

• If you are firing glass in a mold in a shallow kiln chamber (top or side firing), it is not necessary to put a shelf into the kiln. Simply place the mold on four kiln posts (at least 1" high).

• A good rule to remember is: Never open a kiln when its temperature is between 500°F and 1000°F during either the heating or cooling process. This could cause thermal shock.

• Projects should not be placed closer than 1" from the side elements.

• After your project is fired, you can remove it when the temperature reaches 300°F, but be careful—the glass will still be hot!

• Allow your fused enamel piece to remain at room temperature for 18 to 24 hours before washing it by hand or in a dishwasher.

• Metal inclusions in glass must be fired slowly at first. Heat glass at 150°F per hour to 350°F, and hold for 30 minutes. Then proceed to the temperatures given for either manually or digitally controlled kilns.

• If you are using dark-colored fusible glass, decrease the final maturing temperature by 25°F to 50°F. Black glass matures at a lower temperature than white, so be careful when planning your color schemes and firing dark and light glass.

• Dull colors indicate inaccurate firing. Check your cooled project. If it is under-fired, re-fire to the correct temperature.

• If you look into the kiln after enamels have matured, the colors may appear to have changed. However, when the piece has cooled, the colors will return to their natural hue. If sifted enamels look grainy, they may not have matured. Once they are properly fired, the surface of the glass will be shiny.

• If the door of your top loading kiln is heavy, you might consider attaching it to a pulley system.

TROUBLESHOOTING FIRING PROBLEMS

Glass Bubbles
Probable cause:

1. Heating the glass in the kiln too quickly.

2. Air trapped between layers of glass.

3. Grease or dirt between layers of glass.

4. Uneven glass volume.

5. Use of certain textured glass.

Remedy: To reduce or eliminate bubbles in the fired glass, fire the kiln more slowly after the temperature has reached 1200°F. This will allow the trapped air to escape before the edges of the glass are sealed. An alternate method is to heat soak the glass in the kiln for 10 to 20 minutes when the temperature has reached 1200°F. Fire on fiber paper so the air can dissipate.

Since grease or dirt between layers of glass will cause bubbles, keep the glass clean.

Cracking
Probable cause:

1. Heating or cooling the kiln too quickly (the larger or thicker the glass, the more slowly you must heat and cool it).

2. Fusing incompatible glass (buy stained glass tested for fusing compatibility).

3. Opening the kiln between the temperatures of 500°F and 1000°F.

Factors Affecting Firing Results
1. Glass type and color.

2. Kiln type and shape.

3. Heating element location and how close the glass is to it.

4. Thickness and thermal mass of shelf or molds.

5. Thickness and diameter of the work.

6. Thickness variations within the work.

7. Placement within the kiln and available air circulation.

8. Size of the component pieces of glass being heated for fusing.

FACTS ABOUT SLUMPING

Slumping can be defined as the controlled bending of glass under the influence of heat and gravity within a kiln. This is generally done over or into a mold. Molds can be made out of a variety of different materials and can be found at art glass suppliers. (For details, see Chapter Ten.)

When slumping, it is necessary to take into account the shape of the mold, the thickness of the piece, and the degree of heat desired.

Gravity plays a very important role in slumping, especially slumping over a mold as opposed to into a mold. If the shape of the mold dictates that the unbent glass is largely unsupported, the weight of the unsupported glass will pull the glass over the mold more quickly than if only a small portion is unsupported.

A single thin piece of glass will fuse a little faster than a thick piece of glass. Therefore, if you are using a mold, a thick piece of glass will require more hold time in the final segment of the process phase.

OVERFIRING

If the fused piece has been overfired, it could appear frosted, and the edges may be uneven or have sharp projections. Colors may have been burned out as well. To repair the damage, be sure to grind down any sharp edges first. More enamels can be applied to the top layer. You may attempt to re-fire at a lower temperature, around 1450°F.

BUBBLES

If a large bubble occurs, with skill, it can be repaired. Fire the project until the glass is pliable by firing it to a higher temperature (1600°F to 1700°F). Open the kiln door and prick the bubble with a long-handled glass hook tool. Close the door and let the glass melt together. Shut off the kiln as soon as the glass has remelted. This should take only a few minutes. Be sure to wear heatproof gloves and work quickly. The kiln temperature will probably drop by 100°F. Allow the temperature to rise again to 1600°F to see if the glass has remelted properly.

Repairing bubbles is easier to do if you have a side-firing kiln and can easily open the kiln door. However, if you have a top loading kiln, unless the top is opened by a pulley, you might need assistance to lift the top while you are pricking the bubble.

Fiber paper can help to eliminate small bubbles. Use ceramic fiber paper, which

When glass is overfired, the edges can develop sharp projections.

This fused glass disk demonstrates overfired enamels. The fired glass enamels have separated in the center.

This fused enamel plate has devitrified in the firing process, resulting in a dull surface. There are several ways to rectify the problem.

comes in various thicknesses, as an alternative to the kiln wash. Remember to cut the fiber paper to size to fit under your project. Fiber paper lasts for several firings if handled carefully.

If you are firing in a deep kiln chamber (more than 14″ deep), place the mold or shelf on 4″ kiln posts. With more air circulation under the piece, it will fire with fewer bubbles.

CLEANING THE FINISHED PROJECT

Use a mask while doing this cleaning procedure: After lifting the glass from the mold, clean the excess kiln separator or fiber paper from the fused glass. Use a brush to scrape the kiln separator into a bucket of water. Discard the dry mold separator that remains on the mold; it should not be used again.

DEVITRIFICATION

Devitrification is the formation of minute crystals that may occur on some glass surfaces over a certain period of time and at a certain temperature while in the kiln. After firing, the glass may appear hazy, with a matte finish. This haziness sometimes occurs during the fusing process just before the glass becomes molten, when the glass has been left too long in the temperature range between 1350°F and 1475°F.

With new glass manufacturing technology, however, devitrification is less likely to occur on fusible, iridescent, and dichroic glass. To discourage devitrification, especially on float glass, spray or brush an anti-devitrification glaze on the glass surface prior to firing. A fired piece that has devitrified can be re-fired using an anti-devitrification spray.

REMOVING BAKED-ON KILN WASH

Sometimes kiln wash sticks to the underside of a finished piece of glass. Firing glass on kiln shelves or molds that are not completely dry or shelves where the kiln wash has started to deteriorate can lead to problems. Kiln wash can also stick to glass if you over-fire or soak the glass too long in the kiln.

Sandblasting the back of the fused glass is a fast and efficient method of removing baked-on kiln wash. It can also enhance the appearance of the finished project and give it a satin finish. However, if you prefer a shiny finish, you can re-fire the piece.

Another method of removing baked-on kiln wash is to apply a paste of toilet cleanser crystals and water; then scrape the glass with a nylon scrubbing pad or very fine steel wool.

Remember that by firing your piece on thin fiber paper or sifted kiln wash powder, you can eliminate the baked-on kiln wash problem.

CHAPTER TWELVE

Kilns

KILN SELECTION

Today there is a large selection of kilns available in a wide range of prices. A kiln is a serious investment, and time spent during the selection process will prevent needless expense later on. It is important that each person select the appropriate kiln for his or her individual needs and purposes. With so many types, sizes, and brands of kilns with different features, it could be a challenge to make the right decision. Attending classes, visiting kiln dealers, and reading books can help the beginner make a wise choice.

TYPES OF POWER

There are two basic types of kilns: those powered by gas and those powered by electricity. The electrical kilns are usually less expensive to purchase and easier to use than the gas kilns. Because the electrical kilns are more readily available and more widely used by glass artists, the following information will pertain to electrical kilns only.

MANUAL CONTROLLERS

A small kiln with a manual controller can be a wise investment for a beginner because it is less intimidating. Later, when you are more experienced and have an idea of the types of projects you want to create, you can use the smaller kiln for test firings. Check the outside dimensions of the models that interest you. Determine if you have 18" of clearance on all sides from combustible walls.

If you plan to produce large, flat panels and shallow mold tableware, consider a top firing kiln with a shallow chamber. Many artists prefer top firing kilns because they fire projects evenly. Deep molds or tall drape molds will require kilns with a deep chamber. Once you get involved with hot glass, you may find that you require two or three different types and sizes of kilns to serve your needs.

Most kilns come with some type of pyrometer so that you can gauge the temperature in the kiln as the glass is firing. Kilns with manual controllers need to be watched and temperatures adjusted when the pyrometer reaches certain temperatures.

DIGITAL CONTROLLERS

Digital controllers are programmed by the user at the beginning of the firing. The kiln automatically goes through various stages, such as holding at certain temperatures, turning off, and annealing, if needed. However, even with the benefit of a computerized kiln, you need to familiarize yourself with the programs that are best suited for your particular types of projects, including the size, thickness, and type of glass.

The primary criteria for choosing a glass kiln are type of controller desired, cost, electrical power, size and quantity of the pieces to be fired, and types of techniques to be used. John Hohenshelt, President of Paragon Industries (a manufacturer of kilns), gives an overview of various types of kilns. Part of that information is included in the following text.

MORE ABOUT CONTROLLERS

There are three types of controllers used in glass kilns: infinite switches, simple digital controllers, and professional digital controllers. The smaller, simpler kilns designed to plug into normal household outlets tend to have infinite switches and simple digital controllers, while larger, more sophisticated kilns tend to have the more complex controllers. Therefore, the type of controller that is standard on a kiln is what is appropriate for the kiln design.

Infinite Switches
Infinite switches are manual controllers with knobs similar to those on electric ranges or stoves with low, medium, and high or numbered designations. These switches are very basic and inexpensive and a good choice for a beginner. Many of these kilns operate on 110 volts of household current. They do not control the temperature of the kiln; they simply control the amount of time the elements are actually on. They should be used in conjunction with a pyrometer, which is usually connected to the kiln. This is a device that accurately measures the temperature inside the kiln. Infinite switches are not capable of controlling the temperature of a kiln during a hold cycle but are very efficient for small, quick projects.

Simple Digital Controllers
These are designed for beginners and for glass artists of intermediate experience. The controllers can be programmed to heat up, hold, and control the cool down rate for annealing, then turn off automatically. They make firing glass projects very easy. These digital controllers tend to have

few diagnostic tools, can store only one program, and offer few advanced options for more complicated techniques. They are relatively inexpensive and easy to use.

Professional Digital Controllers

These controllers are designed for the intermediate to professional level user. They are more complex to program, offer a wide array of diagnostic tools and advanced options for perfecting the firing, and generally have a connection for use with a computer interface. Professional digital controllers generally have up to 20 segments and can store multiple programs in memory.

Most kilns are constructed of ceramic brick; therefore they are well insulated and cool slowly. Kilns constructed of fiber, however, do require special annealing because they cool very rapidly. Projects under 12″ with only two layers of glass do not require an annealing schedule in a ceramic brick kiln. However, in a fiber brick kiln, they will require annealing.

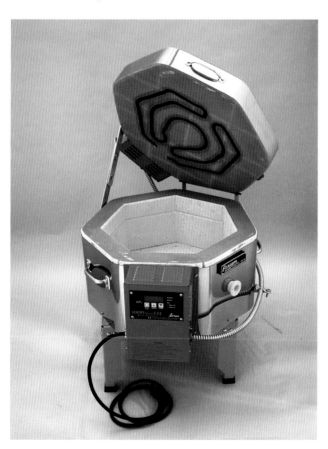

Above: Kiln with top elements. Right: Kiln with top and side elements. Photos courtesy of Paragon Kilns.

TOP AND SIDE HEATING ELEMENTS

Top Elements

This design has been in existence for many years. A major benefit of a top element kiln is that it heats flat glass evenly, and your glass will have an even, shiny surface when fired.

Side Elements

If you heat from the sides only, the outside edge of the glass will heat faster than the middle. This is excellent for small pieces, shallow molds, and jewelry work, but not for large, thick pieces. Side elements produce uniformity of the heat distribution in a kiln for certain projects, such as firing tall molds. In larger, deep kilns with side elements, two or three shelves can be used, provided you are firing similar types of projects and are allowing adequate space between shelves.

Combined Elements

Many designs come with both top and side elements so they can be used for a variety of techniques. Some enable you to fire the elements individually or in combination. These kilns are more versatile, larger, and relatively expensive.

TOP LOADING KILNS

Top loading kilns come in three basic design shapes, in either a polygon, a rectangle, or a square.

Polygon top load kilns are very economical for their size. They have proven themselves over many years. They will fire most types of glass projects very efficiently. The main drawback is they are not conducive to techniques that require the artist to manipulate the glass when it is hot because, when the user opens the lid, all the heat is released. Many of these polygon kilns are made in either top only or top and side element versions.

FRONT LOADING KILNS

Front loading square kilns have a door that opens to one side. These kilns are easy to load and enable you to view your projects easily. The more advanced user can manipulate the glass with tools while the glass is pliable and hot. Some kilns are designed with door safety switches that turn off the elements when the door is opened. These kilns also are designed to permit the user to adjust the amount of heat from the top elements and side elements.

TIP TOP-IC
A small viewing window is an attractive special feature in a kiln. It enables you to keep a watchful eye on your project during the firing process.

Most of the kilns manufactured today are certified to Underwriters Laboratories (UL) specifications or the specifications of equivalent testing agencies. Follow the instruction guidelines regarding placement, power, and safety information. Kilns are safe when used in a proper and responsible manner. Find a kiln that will operate on the electrical service of your building. Consult an electrician and the manufacturer for the exact electrical specifications for the model you want to purchase because you may require additional current.

Once you have purchased your kiln, practice firing small scrap pieces to get acquainted with the features and capabilities. It is important to know your kiln, and to understand how it fires and where the hot areas are in the chamber.

OPTIONAL ACCESSORIES

If you already have a kiln and would like to upgrade it, numerous optional accessories are available. You can purchase computerized portable kiln controllers that come with various features from basic to sophisticated. Other accessories include kiln stands, kiln vents, and pyrometers.

You can buy kiln furniture, such as shelves and posts in various shapes and sizes to fit different kilns. Shelves can vary in composition. Some are lighter in weight than others and can be easier to handle, especially if the shelves are large.

Kiln posts can be placed between shelves or under the bottom shelf. The shelf should be positioned at least 1″ above the kiln floor to allow for air circulation. These posts can also be used under a mold instead of using a shelf.

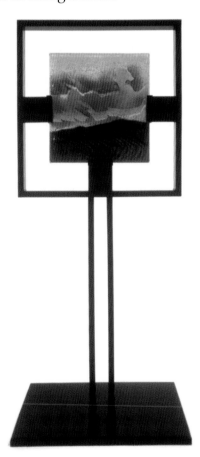

Cathy Coverley

The art glass panel framed on a metal stand was created with fine glass enamel powders laminated between several layers of glass to give dimension to the scene.

Safety in the Work Area

PUT SAFETY FIRST

The following important instructions will help to provide a safer and more efficient working environment. Familiarize yourself with them, and post them in the studio for the benefit of anyone working there. Please always use common sense and remember to put safety first.

HEAT AND FIRE SAFETY

• Floors and surfaces should be made of fire-resistant materials that are easy to mop and sponge clean.

• The stainless steel jacket and some of the other fixtures surrounding the kiln will get hot enough to burn your skin when the kiln is heated, so be careful around a hot kiln.

• The heating coils inside the kiln chamber will cause an electrical shock if touched. Never insert metal instruments into the kiln while it is firing.

• Keep areas around the kiln free of flammable and combustible materials. Make sure that no flammable liquids are stored near your kiln.

• Sufficient air space (18″) should be provided around kilns. Mount a kiln on a stand to allow air circulation under it. Metal stands are best; ceramic tile or brick stands are also acceptable. A heatproof shelf on a metal table will suffice.

• Make sure your kiln is properly set up by a qualified electrician, and be sure the kiln has proper circuit breakers for protection against any electrical malfunctions. It is best to have a separate dedicated circuit for each unit. If you have more than one kiln on the same circuit, run only one at a time.

• Kilns draw a large amount of electrical current, and an extension cord that is not rated for the high current could overheat and cause a fire. If you have moved your kiln, make certain that your plug is firmly in the wall jack and that all the connections are secured and not frayed.

• Fire extinguishers or other approved fire control equipment should be installed. Post and practice emergency fire procedures. Make sure to read over the instructions to ensure that you understand how to use the equipment.

• Work in a well-ventilated area. Provide your kiln with exhaust ventilation, such as a canopy hood, or place the kiln near a window exhaust fan.

• If you work in your garage, back your car out before you start working so that there are no gasoline fumes around.

• Maintain a clear exit route from your work space at all times so that you can escape in case of fire.

• Try not to leave your kiln unattended. If you must leave your kiln, check on it frequently. Even with kilns set on a digital controller, problems have been known to occur.

GLASS SAFETY

• Never grasp large glass sheets by their corners. When carrying large sheets, hold the glass vertically—not horizontally—to prevent it from breaking in your hands.

• When purchasing supplies, allow the shop proprietor to handle and cut large glass pieces from warehouse racks.

• Use a table brush frequently to keep the work surface free of glass chips.

• Always rinse out your grinder and saw water reservoir with running water to remove scum and stagnant water.

• Avoid breathing glass dust. Grind glass wet, and clean up the residue before it dries and becomes dust. The dust is considered toxic.

• Enamel spills should be cleaned up immediately. Use wet cleaning sponges and mops to avoid raising glass and lead dust. This will ensure that the dust is not transferred to other areas.

• Glass and enamel grinding dust are toxic waste. Dispose of these materials properly.

PROTECTIVE CLOTHING AND ACCESSORIES

Burns from kilns are usually a result of not wearing appropriate attire or not paying proper attention to what you are doing. Here are some general rules to help you avoid getting burned:

- Always wear safety glasses to protect your eyes when cutting glass, grinding, or working with powders and frit. When looking into the kiln for extended periods of time, use plastic, green-shaded 2.5 safety glasses with side shields, or grey IR and UV protective glasses.

- If you are going to be working with glass enamels for an extended time, wear a protective mask and use an exhaust fan.

- Make sure to wear heatproof gloves when touching the kiln or removing projects, and always turn off the kiln before reaching into it.

- To prevent cuts, wear comfortable, non-bulky gloves when cutting glass. Stay away from asbestos at all costs.

- Wear a smock or cover-up apron to protect you and your clothing from glass and lead dust. Leave it in the studio so that glass and lead particles are not tracked outside of the work area. Wash and dry work clothes separately from other clothes.

- Avoid wearing synthetic clothing, loose sleeves, or other items that could melt, burn, or catch fire from radiated heat. Wear long-sleeved shirts and pants made of natural fibers such as cotton or wool. Wear closed-toed shoes. Make sure to keep clothing and sleeves away from the work surface.

- Long hair should be tied back.

GENERAL PRECAUTIONS

- Wet-mop or use a HEPA vacuum cleaner regularly to keep dust from irritating your lungs. Sweeping or using an ordinary shop vacuum will simply spread the dust into your breathing air and contaminate your entire workspace.

- Spray products containing solvents should be used with local exhaust ventilation.

- Isolate a work area for mixing chemical powders so that they do not get spread all around your studio. This work area should also have adequate ventilation to help remove airborne dust.

- Never apply enamel powders or frits in or near living or eating areas.

- Do not eat, drink, smoke, or apply makeup while working with glass enamel products. Always wash your hands before eating.

- Never rub your eyes with soiled hands. Keep cuts well covered.

• Read and follow manufacturers' directions and precautions regarding their products. When purchasing chemicals, ask for the Materials Safety Data Sheets.

• Label all chemicals that have been transferred from their original containers.

• Do not allow small children into your studio or work area without supervision. Keep pets away from your work area.

ADDITIONAL ADVICE

• Keep a first-aid kit handy.

• Keep electrical cords and outlets dry.

• If you get burned, keep the affected area immersed in ice-cold water until the pain diminishes, or put an ice cube in a clean cloth and place it on the burned area. If there is any question of a severe burn, contact your doctor immediately or go to an emergency clinic.

• Keep a decorative aloe plant nearby. Use the juice from the leaves as a healing salve.

• When you finish working, wash your hands (not in the kitchen sink, please).

• Don't take toxic materials home with you; leave them in your studio.

CHAPTER FOURTEEN

Artist Profiles

Today, glass art creations not only reflect the artists' inner visions, but their visions are made possible because of new products resulting from the advancement of technology. Such an abundance of materials enables glass artists to create extraordinary concepts never before achievable.

Steve Immerman

This is a 10" round, fused and slumped bowl with an image of an ancient Chinese horse silk-screened in black paint on Bullseye red glass. The rim was iridized black glass, but the iridescent surface was sandblasted off except for the kanji characters in several locations.

JUDITH FINN CONWAY

Judith Finn Conway is a nationally recognized glass artist, writer, and educator who has created with glass for over twenty-five years. Her work has been chosen for the Arts in the Embassies program of the United States Department of State and is shown in galleries nationwide. For the past ten years, she has focused on kiln-formed glass, using frits and powders and complex constructions to create her award-winning glass portals and sculptures.

Judith and her partner, Kevin O'Toole, have a wide range of glass experience and knowledge. They teach classes and workshops on all aspects of fused, cast, and slumped glass in their studio—the Vitrum Studio in the Washington/Baltimore area (www.vitrumstudio.com).

"My work reflects my deep appreciation and love of the landscapes and the environments in which we live," Judith says. "I look to the shapes and colors, the unique lighting and moods of nearby landscapes caught in a brief snapshot during specific times of the year. My background in horticulture and my strong commitment to our obligation to stewardship of the land are compelling forces in my work."

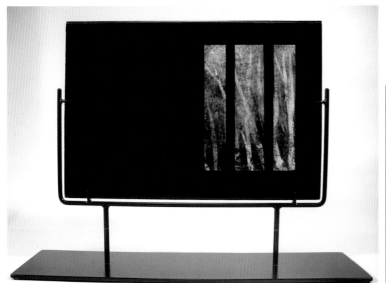

The images were created with glass frit and enamel powders, mica powders, gold foils, and pieces of flat glass cut to shape. These image components were fired, then cut into shape and assembled into the final panel. After firing, the panel was sandblasted and fired again to a semigloss.

JUDITH FINN CONWAY

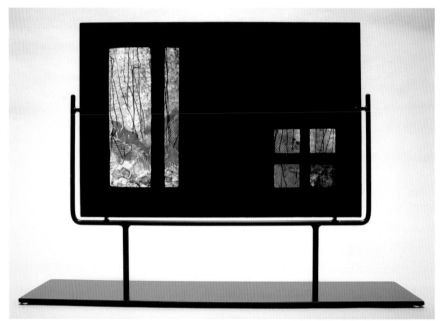

The background panel was created of many 3/8" strips of transparent brown glass placed on edge. These were fired to fuse into a thick transparent background. The transparent scene panels are enhanced by the dark glass background. Simple framing adds a dramatic touch.

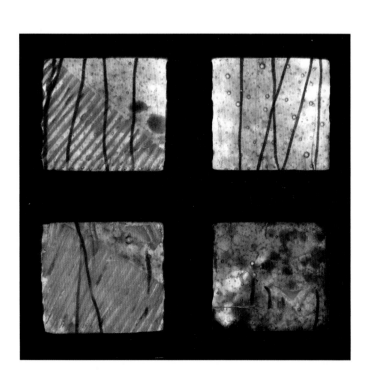

BROCK CRAIG

Brock Craig, an award-winning artist, is engaged in a personal odyssey through the medium of glass art. His current interest is primarily in kiln work, including fused and slumped bowls, sushi trays and platters, torsos, and painted and fired panels. He was a student at the Pilchuck Glass School. His art involves many steps of decorating layers of glass, including sandblasting and layering with gold and silver leaf. The decorated glass then requires several firings. Brock and Avery Anderson have started team-teaching kiln-working techniques throughout the country.

Brock Craig has developed a glass art style that is as spectacular as his shimmering gold and silver foil inclusions. Each bowl incorporates silver and gold leaf that has been shredded, cut, or pulverized.

MICHAEL DUPILLE

Michael Dupille has perfected his complicated glass enamel technique that features imaginative subject matter. He uses the term "Fritology" to describe his style of glass art. Only by firing his decorated glass multiple times can he achieve the complex designs that are seen in his art pieces.

Michael was recently awarded a prestigious commission by the City of New York for a future memorial world trade park. The artist will be designing and constructing an immense glass wall, a water fountain, and glass art panels for the promenade.

An imaginative subject perfected in multiple firings of glass, enamel powders, and frit.

This complex wall panel was created of fused glass, incorporating enamel powders and frit and fired multiple times. The "fence wire" was painted by hand.

STEVE IMMERMAN

Steve Immerman has been working in art glass for twenty-five years and exclusively with kiln-formed glass for the past ten. His training has been a combination of experimenting, studying, and attending multiple comprehensive kiln-forming workshops. His work has been exhibited in the Midwest and on the West Coast, and is in private collections throughout the United States.

Steve has developed a sophisticated style evolving from techniques that include sandblasting, silk-screening, laminating inclusions, and fusing.

The artist grew up in the suburbs of New York City. He began working with stained glass in 1979, and ultimately graduated to kiln-formed glass in 1995.

"I use glass to evoke images and memories of beautiful things and places," he says.

 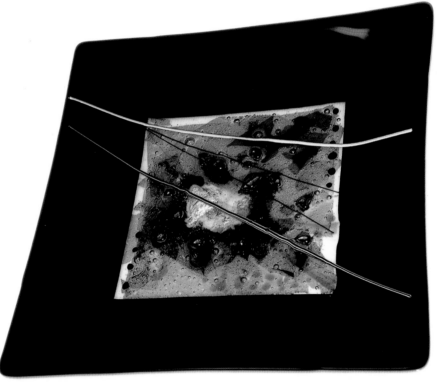

The center of this fused plate has several layers of copper leaf laminated between layers of fusible clear glass. A myriad of bubbles have formed on the copper (see close-up at left). Blue and green frit and hot-worked stringer inclusions add dimension to the art piece.

The plate contains inclusions of silver leaf, frit, and hot-worked stringers laminated within layers of clear fusible glass and black fusible glass.

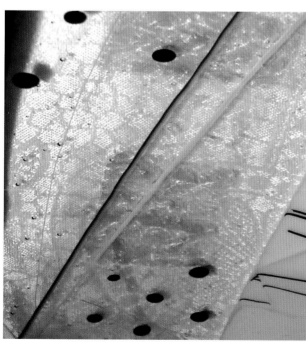

BRUCE LAUGHLIN

One of the early explorers of the potentials of enamel powders and paints, Bruce has always been an innovator, using various techniques in glass. His artistic vision and creativity have taken him from the infancy of modern warm glass to today's hot glass techniques.

Bruce has experimented with practically everything that would fit inside a kiln. He was successfully fusing with Spectrum Glass for many years before the release of their tested compatible glass line. He was also designing and making pieces that contained inclusions in the glass and pieces with decoration between the glass layers.

Bruce is a highly respected hot glass instructor with a world of knowledge to share.

Bruce Laughlin uses his knowledge of diverse techniques to develop many of his own methods, as shown in this silk-screened panel.

The artist creates many of the molds he uses for his line of enamel bowls and platters.

ROBERT LEATHERBARROW

"My approach to assembling pieces involves extensive use of elements," says the artist. "The small pieces are made in advance and later included in larger compositions. These include paper-thin powder wafers, rods, small symbols and patterns, and glass sheet that is cut into strips. When completing a piece, I assemble elements from my stockpile and position or layer them on a textured glass sheet. This construction technique allows me to impart a sense of spontaneity to each piece.

"The final stages in finishing the piece are sandblasting to impart a satin matte finish, and bending the piece into its final shape during a last heating in the kiln.

"I have developed a technique that I call 'crackled texture.' It has become my signature style."

Leatherbarrow's work is created and shaped through multiple firings in an electric kiln. A typical piece requires a minimum of three firings, each of which takes twelve hours.

"I think of a sheet of glass as my canvas, and the colored powders as my paint," he says.

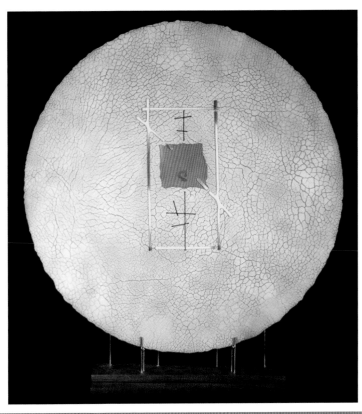

This distinctive round panel was created through a unique process that the artist has developed. His crackle textured effect is achieved by using layers of clear glass and thin layers of enamel powders that are kiln-fired multiple times.

STEVE MADDY

"Multimedia" is a term Steve Maddy has taken to heart. His reverse painted slumped glass plates are created almost opposite from the way you perceive the finished piece. "I paint the detail first, then the secondary detail, then the overall background," he explains.

Steve continues, " I work on a series, find something new and go from there. I really like experimenting with sculpture. I work to make things other people don't make." His dramatic sculptures and unusual patterns are proof enough that his work is in a unique category and not like anyone else's.

Steve Maddy creates dramatic sculptures using 1" clear glass. He uses low fire enamels to paint the fascinating woven patterns of his designs.

MICHEL MAILHOT

Michel Mailhot has been passionate about sculpting glass for the past twenty-five years. He pushes the boundaries of glass thermoforming (cast glass), with results beyond imagination. His inspiration comes from nature—wind, rocks, water—a very organic approach.

Michel is a leader in this area of thermoforming. He uses his artistic talent to create unique pieces in massive sizes, such as 10'-high by 7'-wide sculpture panels from a 4"-thick slab of glass weighing nearly 3000 pounds! He uses enamel powders to enhance his designs.

Challenges from designers and architects bring his skills to life. Whether he works alone as a pure artist, or in collaboration with another professional, Michel always brings out the best in his materials. Sculptures, murals, floors, and lighting fixtures bearing his signature are found around the world and are considered masterpieces.

Michel is affiliated with Think Glass in Montreal, Canada.

This large three-panel divider was made for a private Canadian residence by Michel Mailhot. The glass was created by thermoforming. The colors are fired glass enamels. Photo courtesy of Think Glass, Montreal, Canada.

LESLIE PERLIS

Explosions of color, energetic lines, and fluid forms all describe the work of Leslie Perlis over the last thirty years. Collaborating with client and architect, she creates cutting-edge designs that satisfy the demands of the project as well as her own artistic needs.

"I like to describe my designs as visual expressions of the invisible forces in our lives," Leslie says. "My exhibit/gallery pieces allow me the freedom to express visual interpretations of ideas, feelings, and concepts that are important to me. Once I have my concept, it is challenging to then figure out how to create my ideas in glass. Current explorations in mosaic work allow me to combine all my past experiences with glass, including painting and fusing. I love to experiment with the endless possibilities of glass by inventing new techniques and taking old techniques to new levels."

Leslie is a multitalented glass artist who not only has created her own style but also works successfully in various glass media.

An elaborate free-standing, life-sized glass figure by the artist has a four-sided skirt base. This mixed glass medium sculpture is decorated with rubber stamp impressions using low fire enamel paints.

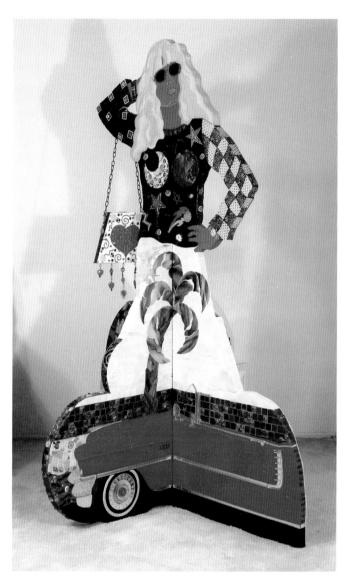

Four scenes embellish the skirt of the three-dimensional glass figure. Combining mosaic, fused, and enamel painted glass techniques enabled the artist to create this striking award-winning glass sculpture.

GIL AND CARMEN REYNOLDS

Gil and Carmen Reynolds own Fusion Headquarters, a hot glass educational and supply center in Portland, Oregon. They have developed many new products for the hot glass industry, including Fuse Master enamel powders.

Gil is recognized as one of the leading innovators in fusing and kiln-forming techniques. He is a contributing writer for various publications. He has also written and produced several books and videos on hot glass techniques.

Gil and Carmen are the coordinators of the Hot Glass Horizons educational seminar program offered in the United States. Their work can be found in many private and public collections around the world. Both have traveled the country teaching seminars on glass fusing, pate de verre, glass casting, and creating with specialty equipment.

This plate was created with fusible glass. The inner square, featuring a geometric glass design, was "grouted" with black enamels. The colorful border was created using medium frit. Enamels mixed with water were applied over the frit. The plate was first fired flat and was then slumped in a mold for the second firing.

Squares of beige glass on red glass were fired upside down on fiber paper. The piece was then decorated with powder and frit and slumped in a metal mold.

Sifted enamel powders over leaves created a shadow image on this plate.

KATHLEEN SHEARD

Kathleen Sheard is a nationally recognized glass artist who creates sensitive and detailed micro-mosaic portraits of wild animals in their natural settings.

Kathleen uses glass frit and glass enamel powders to painstakingly draw the details of animal portraits. Using several layers of glass, she works on a clear glass base and basically builds her work from the bottom layer up. The first layer of detail is created with frit and powders and is then covered with what will be a back layer, and so forth. She has to rely on her studies and notes from test firings to create the imagery she wants, since she cannot see what the piece will look like until after it is fired.

To produce large vessels, Kathleen creates detailed flat panel studies of the subject matter, which are fused flat, then cooled and cleaned. The fused panel is taken to a hot glass studio, where it is heated in a kiln until it is hot enough to be put into the "glory hole." The panel is attached to a blow pipe, heated, and blown out into a shaped vessel. (See photo on the following page.)

Kathleen conducts workshops around the country and is highly respected for her artistic teaching skills and her ability to create realistic wildlife in intricate detail.

Her work is found in both wildlife art and glass art galleries across the country. One of her pieces was included in the 2000 Corning Museum New Glass Review's top 100 innovative glass works of the year.

This whimsical panel demonstrates the versatility of this artist's creativity and ability to portray images in glass enamel art. Through multiple layers of kiln fired glass, powders, and frit, the artist spends many hours developing her scenes.

Sections of this spectacular wildlife scene were pre-fired as separate components. Each section was layered and fired up to four times using fusible glass, enamels, and frit.

This glass vessel is kiln-formed and handblown. First it was layered with powders and frit and fired twice. It was then reheated for a rollup technique.

PAUL TARLOW

When Paul Tarlow began working with glass several years ago, his curiosity about, and fascination with, kiln forming quickly evolved into an obsession.

Paul's work has been displayed at the Austin Glass Fusing Center, where he teaches advanced glass powder techniques, and at the Bullseye Connection Gallery.

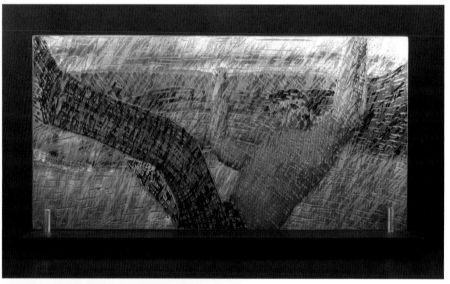

The artist uses float glass with sifted fine enamel to create his glass pictures. After firing, part of the image is then sandblasted and diffused.

Paul spends a lot of his time experimenting and creating with glass powders, enamels, micas, and other materials.

The artist has not only mastered the technique, but he has also developed a unique approach to enamel art.

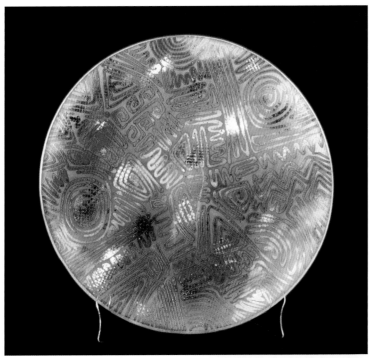

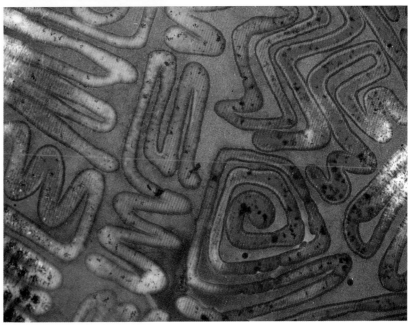

Unusual decorative patterns of enamels were applied to this platter. The artist sandblasted the fired enamel piece to diffuse and enhance the design.

PAT DIACCA TOPP

Pat Diacca Topp is a Wisconsin artist who has received a Bachelor's and a Master's degree in Fine Arts. Her central Wisconsin studio and gallery is now celebrating its thirtieth year. She has specialized in many metal enamel techniques and now creates glass plates and bowls using Carefree Lusters™ that she developed for use on enamels and glass. Pat continues to expand her artistic endeavors in fused and enameled glass and metal.

Her meticulous craftsmanship and design ability have won her many awards in museum and university shows. In the past, she has traveled to many art fairs and shows, but now prefers to spend more time in her studio, producing and experimenting with new techniques.

Decals are available in solid and print patterns and are fired on in a second firing.

150

JANET ZAMBAI

Janet Zambai is a multitalented artist whose specialty is airbrush painting with low fire enamels on sandblasted glass. The result is delicate, and the images appear to be floating in the glass.

Janet owns and operates J Cat Custom Glass Studio in Casper, Wyoming. She has pieces in private collections throughout the United States and around the world. She has close to twenty years' experience, working with most aspects of glass.

This panel was deeply carved by sandblasting clear Baroque glass. Reusche transparent paint was applied with an airbrush, and the piece was fired once.

JANET ZAMBAI

Clear antique glass was used to
create this carved and sandblasted
panel. Fuse Master low fire
transparent paints were applied by
airbrush and fired for lasting beauty.

Coming to Terms with Glass

There are hundreds of terms used in hot glass art; the terms listed here describe only terminology that is pertinent to this text.

AIRBRUSH: A small instrument used for spraying paints. Works with the aid of an air source such as a compressor or air propellant.

ANNEALING: The method of slow-cooling heated glass through the annealing zone to prevent internal stress. Many kilns have computerized controls that automatically regulate temperature in the 800°F to 900°F range, which is typical for annealing small pieces.

ANNEALING POINT: The most efficient temperature at which to anneal a particular glass.

ANNEALING ZONE: The temperature range starting at the softening point and ending at the strain point.

Janet Zambai

Reusche low fire transparent paint was applied by airbrush onto deep-carved, sandblasted Spectrum clear glass. The piece was then fired once.

BLANK: A solid bottom or base layer of glass on which other pieces of glass or enamels are positioned prior to fusing.

BRIDGE: A strip of sanded wood or acrylic approximately 15" long by 1-1/2" high and 1-1/2" wide. It supports the arm and hand above the glass while you are painting.

COEFFICIENT OF EXPANSION (COE): The rate of expansion and contraction when glass is heating and cooling. The expansion of heated glass is measured based on the percentage of change in a glass rod heated to 1°C. The most readily available fusible glass today comes in 90 and 96 COE.

COMPATIBILITY: The absence of stress when different glasses are fused together. Factors that affect glass compatibility are the viscosity (resistance to flow) of a glass and glass expansion characteristics. Expansion affects compatibility throughout the full heating temperature range from annealing point to room temperature.

DECAL SHEETS: Solid color or pattern sheets affixed on a paper backing that can be used on any vitreous surface. These sheets produce a soft, reflective, transparent sheen on a glass surface. After the decal is applied to the glass, it is fired between 1250°F and 1550°F, depending on the glass and decals used.

DEVITRIFICATION: Crystallization in glass, usually occurring as a scum on the surface. This crystallization takes place when glass is held at temperatures slightly below the liquidus temperature—approximately 1400°F for most glasses.

DICHROIC GLASS: Glass having an ultra-thin coating of metal oxides and quartz crystal. The unique characteristic of dichroic glass is that it has a transmitted color and a completely different reflective color. Furthermore, these two colors visually change, depending on your angle of view.

DIGITAL CONTROLLER: A programmable controller with six to eight programs. It offers the user choices with regard to ramp set point and soak segment temperature for any combination of fusing, slumping, soaking, or annealing. The controller can be built into a kiln or purchased separately.

ENAMELS: Substances composed of finely ground colored glasses that are available as transparent or opaque lead-free or lead-bearing powders. The dry powders can be sifted on and laminated between glass surfaces. Very fine powders can be suspended in a liquid medium for painting. Firing temperatures vary depending on the manufacturer.

FIBER BLANKET: A refractory, flexible needled blanket that can be used to insulate warm glass projects when they are removed from the hot kiln.

FIBERGLASS: Synthetic material that can be fired, used between layers of glass and enamels or underneath the glass to achieve an unusual texture effect.

FIBER PAPER: An aluminum silica fiber paper that may be used as a fusing surface in place of shelf primer or to provide surface relief. Fiber paper comes in various thicknesses. When fired under glass, it imparts a subtle matte finish to a glass surface.

FLOAT GLASS: Often referred to as "window glass," it is a smooth sheet of glass with two slightly different surfaces, one having what is referred to as a "tin side." Float glass results from the following process: As molten glass flows from the furnace during manufacture, it floats across the surface of a bath of molten tin. The temperature is lowered as the glass moves across the tin.

FRIT: Glass that has been melted, cooled, and crushed or ground. These small granules of glass range from fine powder to grains of rock-salt size and are available in opaque and transparent colors.

FUSE: The process of heat-bonding glass together, usually in a kiln.

FUSIBLE GLASS: Glass of different colors and types that have been factory tested to be "fusing compatible" to each other. Only a few companies manufacture such glass, and it is usually marked as such.

GOLD OR SILVER LEAF (FOIL): Very thin sheets of precious metals used between layers of glass and enamels to achieve special effects.

GOLD OR SILVER LIQUID: Specially designed products for decorating glass objects. These precious-metal oil-based paints provide a rich, elegant finish. They can be applied by brush, outlining pen, airbrush, stamp, or other methods.

HAIKE BRUSH: A natural, soft-bristled brush used to apply fluids such as shelf primer (resist) and other resistant materials because of its absorbent and retentive qualities.

HOLDING AGENTS (Klyr-Fire): Water-based liquid used to hold enamels in place on the glass until it is fired.

HOLD TIME: The amount of time a kiln is held at a steady temperature, either manually or by computer controller.

IRIDESCENT GLASS: Glass flash-fired with a thin layer of metallic crystal. Iridescent glass has a shimmering rainbow surface effect, resembling a film of soft color on water.

KILN: An insulated chamber, either brick-lined or fiber-insulated, used to fuse glass or bake and fire ceramics. Firing temperatures vary from 1200°F to 2400°F.

KILN POSTS: Posts made from cordierite, a low thermal expansion calcine type of refractory clay. Cordierite has a heat tolerance of over 2150°F. Smooth and flat, it will accept shelf primer to keep glass from sticking to the shelf. The posts are used to lift the shelf off the floor of the kiln, as well as to separate shelving within the kiln.

KILN WASH: A high-temperature powder resist that is usually mixed with water and applied to the surface of a kiln shelf or mold to prevent hot glass from sticking.

LAVA CLOTH: A fusible fiberglass fabric that comes in several texture styles. It imparts a texture to a fused glass surface when it is placed under the glass or on top of the glass during firing.

LINE SIFTERS: A sifter specially made and used to sift a very fine line or dots of enamel (80-mesh) particles. Available in two size openings—1/16" and 1/32".

LUSTER DECALS: A paper backing holding metallic oxides in an organic solvent. Upon firing, the organic binders volatilize, leaving an extremely thin layer of metal oxides fused to the glass surface. For best results, laminate between glass.

LUSTER POWDER: A dry powder applied to a glass surface to achieve a "metal flake" or "sparkle" appearance. Supplied as a dry powder, this product can be mixed with water, or with oil-based media, or laminated between glass layers.

MATURE: A term used to describe the desired fired state of enamel or glass. If fired beyond the maturation point, glass is said to be "overfired"; if below, "underfired."

MICA: Powders or flakes of natural minerals that can be added to glass enamels for sparkle. For best results, laminate between two pieces of glass or use with a medium.

MOLD: A form made of a refractory material or metal with which glass can be shaped by slumping into or draping over.

NOODLES: Colored rods of fusible flat glass that are shaped like fettuccine noodles. They are approximately 1/4" wide and up to 18" long.

OUTLINING PEN: A metal instrument with a small well receptacle that can be filled with liquid enamels or gold or silver paints. This pen is used for writing, outlining, or drawing fine details.

PATE DE VERRE: A process whereby crushed glass is fused in a mold.

PYROMETER: A temperature regulator usually built into a kiln for firing control. The pyrometer indicates the temperature of the glass during the firing process.

SANDBLASTING: A mechanism that uses a blast of air carrying sand at a high velocity to etch or cut glass or metal surfaces.

SHEET COPPER (nonadhesive): Pure metal sheeting that can be embossed and cut into designs and fired between layers of glass and enamel for special effect. Most commonly used is .002- gauge.

SHELF PRIMER: Kiln wash applied by brush or airbrush to kiln shelves and molds to prevent glass from adhering during firing.

SIDE FIRING KILN: A kiln with the elements placed around the sides of the interior chamber.

SILK-SCREENING: Using a stencil to impose a design on a screen of silk or other fine fabric. Blank areas are coated with an impermeable substance, and a printing medium such as liquid enamel is forced through the cloth onto the printing surface.

SOAK: Holding glass in the kiln at a predetermined temperature for a specific amount of time.

This is an example of silk-screening an enamel emulsion onto a glass disk.

STACKERS: Accessories used in a kiln for stacking and separating molds of the same size and shape.

STENCIL: A design cut out of metal, paper, or plastic, through which a powder form of glass enamel can be sifted. Ready-made commercial stencils are available.

STRAIN POINT: The lower end of the annealing range.

STRINGER: A fine, thin fusible glass thread (less than 1/16" in diameter). Stringers are often a by-product of glass casting and are often used in fusing for fine detail work.

TEXTURE FIRE: Fusing glass to the point at which it is well bonded but there is still texture on the surface. This is a lower temperature activity than full fuse.

THERMAL SHOCK: The cracking of glass caused by rapid or uneven heating or cooling temperatures.

TIN SCOPE LAMP (Short wave UV light): A battery-powered detector used to determine the tin side of a sheet of float glass (window glass). The tin side shows up foggy (slightly reflective); the reverse side shows up clear.

TOP FIRING KILN: A kiln with heating elements placed in the top of the firing chamber.

VISCOSITY: A fluid's internal resistance to flowing. It is the rate at which glass flows when heated.

Additional Resources

WEBSITES

For additional glass, firing, and fusing information that is constantly being updated, refer to the following glass manufacturers' websites.

Bullseye Glass Co.
www.bullseyeglass.com

Spectrum Glass Company, Inc.
www.spectrumglass.com

Uroboros Glass Studio
www.uroboros.com

MAGAZINES

These publications have excellent hot glass information. They can be purchased from some glass retailers, and subscriptions are available.

Glass Art Magazine
P.O. Box 260377
Highlands Ranch, CO 80163
www.glassartmagazine.com

Glass Craftsman Magazine
P.O. Box 678
Richboro, PA 18954
www.glasscraftsman.com

Glass Patterns Quarterly
8300 Hidden Valley Rd.
Westport, KY 40077
www.glasspatterns.com

Stained Glass News
P.O. Box 310
Ada, MI 49301
www.sgnpublishing.com

CONFERENCES AND WORKSHOPS

Workshops in hot glass are available at the following national conferences.

BECon - Bullseye's Kiln Glass Conference
(Also year-round classes)
Portland, OR
www.bullseyeconnectiongallery.com

Glass Craft & Bead Expo
Las Vegas, NV
www.glasscraftexpo.com

Glass Horizons
Newberg, OR
www.hotglasshorizons.com

Skillfest
Allentown, PA
www.skillfest.net

References

Anderson, Harriette. *Kiln-fired Glass*. Chilton Book Company, Radnor, PA, 1970.
An informative tutorial offering directions for decorating glass with glass enamels, silkscreening design, and more.

Bergsma, Mary. *Kiln-fired Glass*. Thompson Enamel, Highland Park, IL, 1983.
For projects using Thompson Enamel powders with window glass.

Eberle, Bettina. *Creative Glass Techniques: Fusing, Painting, Lampwork*. Lark Books, Asheville, NC, 1997.
Well-defined book with many creative project ideas.

Elskus, Albinas. *The Art of Painting on Glass*. Charles Scribner's Sons, New York, NY, 1980.
Well-written text with information on traditional low fire paint techniques.

Halem, Henry. *Glass Note: A Reference for the Glass Artist*. Franklin Mills Press, Kent, OH, 1996.
An informative and comprehensive guide on various aspects of hot glass.

Home Decorating Institute. *Sponging, etc*. Creative Publishing International, Inc., Minnetonka, MN, 1996.
Booklet on innovative approaches to applying non-fire paints. Useful ideas for applying enamels on glass.

Kahn, Sherrill. *Creating with Paint: New Ways, New Materials*. Martingale & Company, Woodinville, WA, 2001.
A creative and colorful book on how to apply non-fire paint to various surfaces.

Kahn, Sherrill. *Creative Stamping with Mixed Media Techniques*. North Light Books, Cincinnati, OH, 2003.
A beautiful and fascinating guide to using decorative stamps with non-fire paints. Good ideas to use for applying enamels tp glass.

Kaiser, Petra. *Introduction to Glass Fusing*. Wardell Publications, Fort Lauderdale, FL, 2003.
A well-presented fusing project book for beginners. Includes information on carving fiber board for molds.

Kervin, Jim, and Dan Fenton. *Pâte de Verre and Kiln Casting of Glass*. Glass Wear Studios, Livermore, CA, 1997.
A comprehensive text on three-dimensional glass art with detailed technical information.

Larson, Vicki, and Shirley Miller. *With Brush in Hand*. Loew-Cornell, Teaneck, NJ, 2002.
A great guide for learning more about brushes, brush strokes, and how to paint.

Lundstrom, Boyce. *Glass Casting & Moldmaking: Glass Fusing, Book Three*. Vitreous Publications, Inc., Colton, OR, 1989.
Directed to the more experienced hot glass artist. Well-organized information on pate de verre and glass casting.

Lundstrom, Boyce, and Daniel Schwoerer. *Glass Fusing, Book One*. Vitreous Publications, Inc., Colton, OR, 1983.
Excellent text for beginners in hot glass, although some information may be outdated.

Reynolds, Gil. *The Fused Glass Handbook*. Fusion Headquarters, Inc., Portland, OR, 1987.
Considered by many to be the basic text on fusing.

Rossol, Monona. *The Artist's Complete Health and Safety Guide,* Second Edition. Allworth Press, New York, NY, 1996.
A must for every craftsperson.

Walker, Brad. *Contemporary Warm Glass: A Guide to Fusing, Slumping, and Related Kiln-Forming Techniques*. Four Corners International, Inc., Clemmons, NC, 2000.
Comprehensive information; an important addition to a glass person's library.

Weiner, Kay Bain. *Glass Enameling*. Eastman Publishing, Carlsbad, CA, 1994.
A beginner's step-by-step book. Project-oriented, with patterns.

Manufacturers

Listed below are selected manufacturers of glass and related equipment and supplies used in the industry. Although most manufacturers do not sell directly to the consumer, they can direct you to a local supplier. Generally, however, the products mentioned in this book are available at hot glass suppliers.

Brushes

Loew-Cornell, Inc.
563 Chestnut Ave.
Teaneck, NJ 07666

Stamps (rubber)

Impress Me
17116 Escalon Dr.
Encino, CA 91436

Glass, Frit, and Powders

Bullseye Glass Co.
3722 SE 21st Ave.
Portland, OR 97202

CBS
Coatings By Sandberg, Inc.
856 N. Commerce St.
Orange, CA 92867
(Dichroic glass and frit)

Spectrum Glass Company, Inc.
P.O. Box 646
Woodinville, WA 98072

Uroboros Glass Studio
2139 N. Kerby Ave.
Portland, OR 97227

Enamels and Paints

Fusion Headquarters, Inc.
P.O. Box 69312
Portland, OR 97201
(Enamels, molds, kilns, and supplies)

Glassline
A Division of Clay Art Center, Inc.
2636 Pioneer Way East
Tacoma, WA 98404
(Outlining paint)

Hoevel Manufacturing
2320 Abbot Kinney Blvd.
Venice, CA 90291
(Sheet copper, outlining pens, and Thompson Enamel products)

Reusche & Co.
1299 H St.
Greeley, CO 80631

Thompson Enamel
P.O. Box 310
Newport, KY 41072

Unique Glass Colors
P.O. Box 20
Logansport, LA 71049
(Liquid enamels, molds)

Kilns

Evenheat Kiln, Inc.
P.O. Box 399
6949 Legion Rd.
Caseville, MI 48725

Jen-Ken Kilns
3615 Ventura Dr. W
Lakeland, FL 33811

Olympic Kiln
6301 Button Gwinnett Dr.
Atlanta, GA 30340

Paragon Industries
2011 South Town East Blvd.
Mesquite, TX 75149

Skutt Ceramic Products, Inc.
6441 SE Johnson Creek Blvd.
Portland, OR 97206

Fusible Decals

ProFusion
6308 W. Port Royale Ln.
Glendale, AZ 85306

Thompson Enamel
P.O. Box 310
Newport, KY 41072

Molds

Best Mix Products
1628 N. Columbia Blvd.
Portland, OR 97217

Future Forms
Division of Glasstudio-West
999A Cattlemen Rd.
Sarasota, FL 34232

Kaiser-Lee
3732 E. 21st Pl.
Cape Coral, FL 33904
(Fiber board)

Full Selection Suppliers

Bullseye Glass Co.
3722 SE 21st Ave.
Portland, OR 97202

Fusion Headquarters
15500 NE Kincaid Rd.
Newberg, OR 97132

Miscellaneous

Lava Cloth
P.O. Box 160
Suncook, NH 03275

Contributors

Avery Anderson
Anderson Glass Art
P.O. Box 1480
Veneta, OR 97497

Judith Finn Conway
Vitrum Studio, Inc.
6824 Industrial Dr., Studio #105
Beltsville, MD 20705

The Corning Museum of Glass
Five Museum Way
Corning, NY 14830

Cathy Coverley
Phoenix Glass
4474 Orchard Ave.
San Diego, CA 92107

Brock Craig
Craig Studios
1634 East 6th, #401
Vancouver, BC V5N 1P3, Canada

Michael Dupille
Sunset Grove LCC
10838 Marine View Dr. SW
Seattle, WA 98146

Dan Fenton
Fenton Glass Studio
851 81st Ave., #201
Oakland, CA 94621-2535

Tony Glander
311 Kent Square Rd.
Studio 112
Gaithersburg, MD 20878

John Hohenshelt
Paragon Industries, L.P.
2011 S. Town East Blvd.
Mesquite, TX 75149

Steve Immerman
Steve Immerman Kilnformed Glass
120 Marston Ave.
Eau Claire, WI 54701

Darlene Johnson
Judy Lee
Fused Fantasies
7416 8th Ave. NW
Bradenton, FL 34209

Petra Kaiser
Kaiser Glass Design Studio
3732 SE 21st Pl.
Cape Coral, FL 33904

Peggy Karr
Peggy Karr Glass, Inc.
100 Washington St.
Randolph, NJ 07869

Pauline Kinnman
Margot Clark
Juanita Niemeyer
Unique Glass Colors
P.O. Box 20
Logansport, LA 71049

R. Bruce Laughlin
310 Hackmatack St.
Manchester, CT 06840

Robert Leatherbarrow
Leatherbarrow Glass Studio
128 Parkridge Pl. SE
Calgary, Alberta T2J 4V9, Canada

Steve Maddy
Pattern Bank
2876 Barbour Dr.
San Diego, CA 92154

Michel Mailhot
Think Glass
10741 Georges-Pichet
Montreal, Quebec H1G 5K4, Canada

Peter McGrain
McGrain Glass International
207 Maple St.
Bingen, WA 98605

Annette Laabs Paajanen
Annette Paajanen Fused Glass
2314 Falcon Dr.
West Linn, OR 97068

Leslie Perlis
955 Cornish Dr.
San Diego, CA 92107

Jayne Persico
J.P. Glassworks Studio
50 N. Vine St.
Hazleton, PA 18201

Carmen Reynolds
Gil Reynolds
Fusion Glass Works
15500 NE Kincaid Rd.
Newberg, OR 97132

Nancy Duns Rich
P.O. Box 9309
Marina Del Rey, CA 90295

Howard Sandberg
CBS
Coatings By Sandberg, Inc.
856 N. Commerce St.
Orange, CA 92867

Robert J. Schmidt
Jennifer Yalch
Karen Yan
Schmidt Stained Glass
1324 Kroker Dr.
Ambridge, PA 15003

Linda K. Scott
The Gingham Lady Glass
1705 Running Branch Rd.
Edmond, OK 73013

Kathleen Sheard
HC60 Box 3315
Haines, AK 99827

Paul Tarlow
IZM Studio, LLC
P.O. Box 1537
Cedar Park, TX 78630

Pat Diacca Topp
The Topp Shop & Gallery
709 W. 5th St.
Marshfield, WI 54449

Kay Bain Weiner
7447 Via de Fortuna
Carlsbad, CA 92009

Janet Zambai
J Cat Custom Glass Studio
6753 Terrace Dr.
Casper, WY 82604

Biography

Kay Bain Weiner's passion for painting in oils, watercolors, and acrylics throughout the years has enhanced her appreciation of painting on glass with enamels. Kay first began glass enameling 38 years ago when she studied in New York under the guidance of world-famous glass enamelist Maurice Heaton. Her long friendship with Peggy Karr, another renowned glass enamelist, inspired her to write her 1996 book, *Glass Enameling*.

A noted designer, Kay has worked in stained, fused, and enameled glass for many years and has undertaken numerous commissions for private residences and public buildings. She has been a demonstrator and consultant for Canfield Quality Solder for 20 years and is the president of Eastman Corporation and Eastman Publishing.

Kay has taught hundreds of workshops in the United States and abroad. She is a presenter at various trade shows and conferences. She is the author of twelve other books on glass art and design and has also written and produced several related audio and video cassettes. Her book *Creative Designing: Innovative Glass Art* won the 2003 People's Choice Award for Best New Product at the Art Glass Show, an international trade show. Kay is the innovator and developer of various techniques, tools, and color agents used throughout the glass industry.

Kay lives with her husband in Carlsbad, California.